# NORTHUMBERLAND
## AND THE LAND OF THE PRINCE BISHOPS

Give us the North - And keep your level shires -
The high, wet North lit by a gleam of spring;
And all aglow with opalescent fires;
Great fells and waters glittering.
Down from the heights which stand the whole year round;
Star-gazing in the clouds.

Oxland

# NORTHUMBERLAND
## AND THE LAND OF THE PRINCE BISHOPS

— ED GELDARD —

breedon **books**
PUBLISHING

First published in Great Britain in 2008 by

The Breedon Books Publishing Company Limited

Breedon House, 3 The Parker Centre,

Derby, DE21 4SZ.

A catalogue record for this book is available from the British Library.

ISBN 978-1-85983-618-7

Printed and bound in China.

# CONTENTS

# FOREWORD
## BY HIS GRACE THE DUKE OF NORTHUMBERLAND

There are few areas in the United Kingdom with such a beautiful landscape or such a wealth of cultural, military, industrial and religious history than far North-East England. Ed Geldard's wonderful photographs and finely researched commentary give us a broad view of this heritage and reflect his passion for the area. It shows us familiar views, buildings and monuments both ancient and modern, but it also enlightens the native and visitor alike to the wealth of innovation, design, architecture and natural forces that have carved this unique part of Britain.

Despite living in Northumberland for most of my life, I have learnt much from reading this book, including fascinating details from my own back yard! I had no idea, for instance, that the sleepy seaside village of Alnmouth was once a small sea-port, 'famous for all kinds of wickedness', and was attacked by pirates and ceased to be a port when the river changed its course after a great storm in 1806.

This is a fascinating guide to the region and an album of great beauty, with images to savour at leisure.

# INTRODUCTION

'The Saxon is not like us Normans:

His manners are not so polite.

But he never means anything serious till he talks about justice and right.

When he stands like an ox in the furrow with his solemn set eyes on your own

And grumbles, "This isn't fair dealing"; my son, leave the Saxon alone.'

*Norman and Saxon*, Rudyard Kipling

It was the Norman conquerors who first divided this region into an earldom north of the River Tyne and the Palatine of Durham ruled by 'Prince Bishops' in the south. The Palatinate has its basis in Anglo-Saxon times when kings would confer gifts of land on the bishops. Powerful though he was, William the Conqueror could not crush these two counties. Both were to be omitted from the *Domesday Book,* and he had to be content with setting up garrisons in his attempt to curb the Scots.

Both Northumberland and Durham have a rich historical heritage. It is a heritage set in a land of contrasts. Long after the Roman legions had left, Northumbria became the cradle of Christianity, and by the beginning of the seventh century it had become a federation of two Angel kingdoms, Bernicia, which stretched from the Forth to the Tyne, and Deira, from the Tyne to the Humber. It was known as North Humber Land, meaning land north of the Humber. According to Bede: 'From the Angles, are descended, all race of the Northumbrians, that is, of those nations that dwell on the north side of the River Humber'.

Northumberland is the most northerly county in England and it is an odd fact that you can find yourself farther north in England than in the Lowlands of Scotland. It is also the most sparsely populated; in fact there are five times as many sheep as people living in Northumberland. The erratically drawn border was constantly involved in border warfare at a time when it had more castles to the mile than any other region. The Normans were prodigious builders. Not only did they erect massive stone castles, but they also replaced most of the churches with equally commanding ecclesiastical edifices in stone. It can be safely said that their great building drives of the late 11th and early 12th century were designed, in part, to impress their superior Norman technology and their permanence of their rule on the English. Numerous other fortified buildings known as bastles and pele towers complement these.

Northumberland is the land of castles. A register of 1415 listed 37 large castles and 78 smaller ones. In the 1514 survey, in which only part of the county was covered, no fewer than 120 castles were scheduled. Many have now disappeared and many more are reduced to a heap of stones, but even today there are still some 60 or 70 castles, both large and small, which pepper the Northumbrian countryside, making it a historian's paradise. Alnwick, home of the powerful Percys; Bamburgh, with its mediaeval appearance; Chillingham, which had a particularly violent history; and the historic ruins of Dunstanburgh and Warkworth are just a few of the strongholds which have contributed to the region's history. Over the years Northumberland has also had its share of famous people, including names such as William Turner, writer of the first botanical work in the English language; the naval hero Lord Collingwood; Earl Grey; John Scott the Lord Chancellor; wood-engravers and artists like Beswick, the Dalziel brothers and Clennell; engineers such as Lord Armstrong and the architect Dobson.

Durham, the other northern county, has seen many changes. The Romans came, and so did the Normans. The Prince Bishops ruled and coal was discovered. Industry boomed and then declined. The county stretches from the Pennine Hills, which form the backbone of northern England, to the North Sea, 45 miles to the east. The rivers Tyne and Tees form its northern and southern boundaries, and within this area of just over 1,000 square miles live two million people.

As well as Durham Cathedral, the county is, perhaps, best known for its contribution to Britain's industrial history. It was the birthplace of the railway, and its shallow coal seams were worked long before seams in other parts of the country. But it is not a heavily industrialised area, nor did its history start with the age of the steam engine. Long before the Industrial Revolution events were beginning to leave their mark on the county. The Saxons built churches, the Vikings raided the monasteries and the Romans built forts.

A visitor to the county does not have to go far to find evidence of its interesting past. There are Roman remains, churches, castles, historic houses, market towns and monuments. Three years after the Norman Conquest, William the Conqueror laid waste to the county and invested in the Bishop of Durham a great deal of power. In this County Palatine the Prince Bishops of Durham were to rule; in all but name they were kings, a force designed to deter Scottish incursions into this part of border country. For many centuries they were to hold ecclesiastical and political power over the Palatinate of Durham, the area between the rivers of the Tees and Tyne, as well as land in Northumberland. They lived in state, held their own court, raised their own armies, collected taxes and ran a mint. They also owned a number of very large estates and the richest coal mines in the county. Henry VIII finally brought to an end the autonomy of the Prince Bishops after the failed rebellion known as the Pilgrimage of Grace from Durham, and withdrew all their powers.

With the importance of the Bishops diminished, the position of the nobility was strengthened and families such as the Lumleys and Percys began to dominate the county.

West Durham's high moorlands are pierced by the headstreams of the Derwent, Tees and Wear. Teesdale, with its characteristic whitewashed farm buildings, has long inspired artists such as Turner and Cotman. The Dales, which make up one third of the county, offer some of the country's finest scenery; rugged upland blends with impressive waterfalls. At High Force the River Tees hurls 70ft over massive rocks to form the largest waterfall in England and to the north is Weardale, once the hunting ground of the Prince Bishops. Today quiet moorland roads open up to give panoramic views and the A689 road from Killhope to Nenthead is the highest classified road in England, rising to over 2,000ft. In June the second-oldest rowing regatta in the country is held in Durham and, in spite of the closure of the pits, the brass bands (once the pride of the mining communities) still attend their annual Gala.

These two counties have enough to satisfy the needs of everyone. You may walk with the Romans along Hadrian's Wall, kneel where St Aidan knelt at the very cradle of Christianity, or hunt with the Prince Bishops. The horizons are far, the views wide.

Ed Geldard, 2007

# ACKNOWLEDGEMENTS

This book is for the people of Northumberland and Durham in the hope that its contents may add interest to their wanderings in two of England's finest counties. As with any such book, there will for various reasons be omissions, and in this respect I would ask the reader's indulgence.

I would like to express my sincere thanks to all of the people who helped enhance my knowledge of Northumberland, especially: Brother Damien of Holy Island; Dave Burleigh of Longframlinton Small Pipes; Dave Bullock of Hardy's; Don Bennett, John Brown and Alan Stott of Durham; the Trustees of Bellingham Heritage Centre; English Heritage; Cedric Iley; Denise Robertson; Richard Stewart; James McCleod; Stephen Ward for the sketch and Gary and Camille Craven for their immeasurable IT help.

Most important of all is the debt I owe to Mag, without whose help this book would have remained an unfulfilled dream.

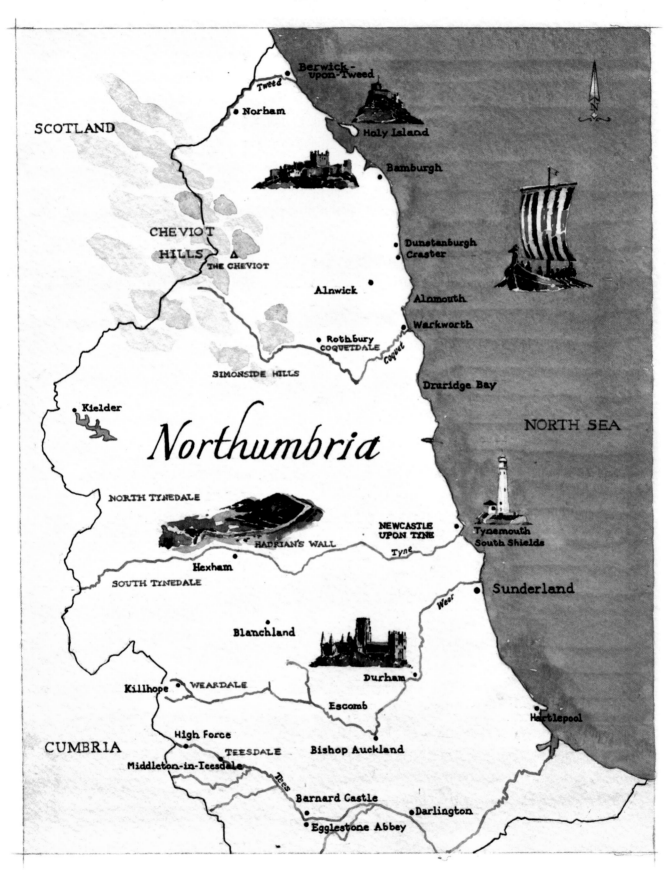

Barnard Castle.

## BARNARD CASTLE

This ancient fortress, whose imposing ruins occupy a rock outcrop on the north bank of the Tees, appears to rise almost vertically from the river edge. Bernard de Baliol first fortified the site in the early part of the 12th century, and beneath its towers the town of Barnard Castle sprang into existence. Throughout the turbulent Middle Ages the castle's ownership was subject to dispute between the Bishops of Durham and other various owners. In 1296 Anthony Beck, Bishop of Durham, seized the castle as part of his Palatinate, occupying it until 1301. Sir Henry Vane unroofed and dismantled the castle in 1630 to provide material for the rebuilding of Raby Castle, and the gradual and progressive decay over the centuries has effected the demolition of all but the outer shell.

## THE BUTTERY: BARNARD CASTLE

Named after its founder, Bernard de Baliol, the mediaeval market town of Barnard Castle is one of the most historic in Britain. The town, which grew up outside the castle, has two main thoroughfares: the cobbled Market Place with its two-tiered Market Hall, erected in 1747 by Thomas Breaks, a native of Barnard Castle, and Galgate. The building is octagonal in shape and the lower storey, a

11

circular colonnaded veranda, was used by butter and egg sellers on market days, the inner part of the building being used as a prison. A room in the upper storey was used for administration purposes and the meetings of magistrates. Galgate, or Gallowgate, according to old maps, is where the ancient town of Marwood stood prior to Barnard Castle. The street is supposed to derive its name from when it was the execution site of the Halifax gibbet, used for the decapitation of criminals by the barony. In 1838 Charles Dickens stayed at the King's Head Hotel to gather material for his novel *Nicholas Nickleby*. Across from the hotel was the shop of Thomas Humphreys, the clock maker whose name Dickens used in *Master Humphrey's Clock* after making his acquaintance when calling to enquire the time of day. Two bullet holes in the weathervane are said to have been made in 1804 by a gamekeeper and

The Buttery, Barnard Castle.

soldier contesting each other's marksmanship. They stood outside the Turk's Head public house and took it in turns to shoot at the vane from a hundred yards away.

## BOWES MUSEUM: BARNARD CASTLE

A short distance from the market place, in an English rural setting, stands a 19th-century French chateau known as the Bowes Museum. It was designed by Jules Pellechett for John Bowes, son of the Earl of Strathmore, and his French wife Josephine, Countess of Montalbo. Their intention at first was to erect the museum at Calais, but ultimately Barnard Castle was chosen, the place having for centuries been connected with the Bowes family. In 1869 the foundation stone was laid without ceremony but, because of some difficulty regarding the legality of the proposed building, operations

Bowes Museum, Barnard Castle.

were suspended until the passing of the Public Park, Schools, and Museums Act of 1871. It opened in 1892 and houses a fascinating display of paintings, furniture and ceramics. Among the most famous painters represented are Hogarth, Reynolds, El Greco, Goya, Murillo and Snyders. One of the more remarkable exhibits is a life-size automaton of a silver swan, which moves its head and appears to take a fish from the water and swallow it. Unfortunately both John and Josephine had died by the time their dream of a museum was realised.

## BLAGRAVES HOUSE: BARNARD CASTLE

Descending The Bank from the Market Cross, you arrive at a narrow four-storey gabled Tudor house known as Blagraves House. It was here, on 24 October 1648, that Oliver Cromwell was entertained by the inhabitants of Barnard Castle with 'burnt wine' and 'short cakes'. The following day he set out for Richmond and did not return north till after King Charles's head had fallen on the scaffold. The building, with its low-beamed ceilings and large open fires, is now a restaurant.

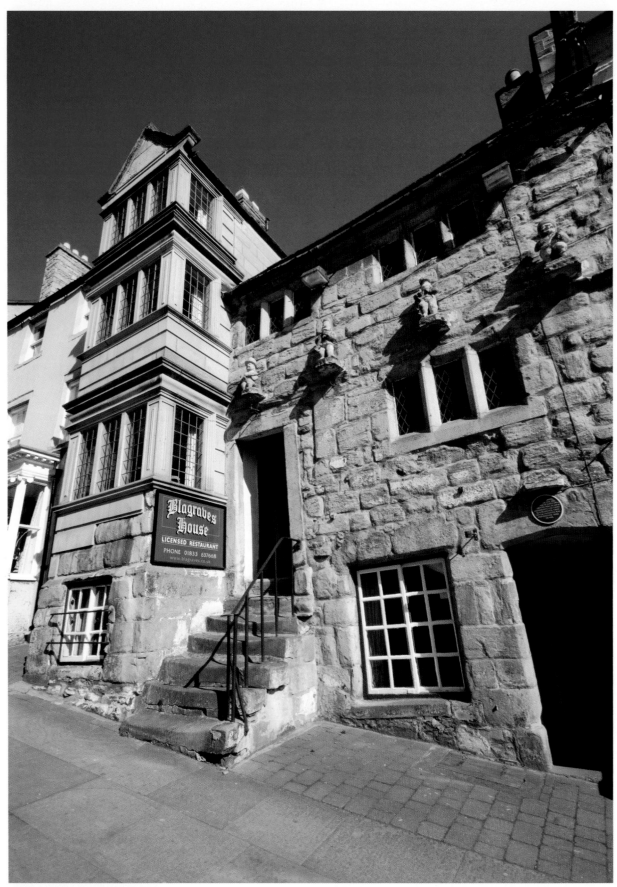

**Blagraves House, Barnard Castle.**

Rokeby Park, Barnard Castle.

## ROKEBY PARK: BARNARD CASTLE

In December 1731 the architect Sir Thomas Robinson wrote to his father-in-law with a report on his first venture, a house he had designed for himself. The house he was referring to was Rokeby, the setting for Sir Walter Scott's romantic ballad. Scott was a friend of John Sawrey Morritt, who acquired the property in 1769, and it was to Scott that Morritt later wrote, telling him of a painting he had purchased. The work by Velasquez showed a beautiful woman, with her back to the artist, gazing at herself in a mirror. In his letter he expressed his concern over the hanging of the picture. He wrote: 'I have been all morning pulling about my pictures and hanging them in new positions to make room for my fine picture of Venus's backside by Velasquez which I have at length exalted over my chimney piece in the library. It is an admirable light for the painting, and shows it in perfection, whilst by raising the said backside to a considerable height the ladies may avert their downcast eyes without difficulty, and connoisseurs steal a glance without drawing in the said posterior as a part of the company.' The picture, known as the 'Rokeby Venus', now hangs in the National Gallery and a copy hangs in Rokeby itself.

Mortham Tower, Rokeby Park.

## MORTHAM TOWER: ROKEBY PARK

The tower house in Durham is rare. Tower houses share a common ancestry with Reivers as they stand on the southern fringe of the Reiver country. Standing close to Rokeby Hall, Mortham Tower in Teesdale is the county's most southerly outpost of its kind. The original pele tower became the core of a Tudor house of great scenic beauty. Originally the tower protected a different entity, that of the village of Mortham. Local records show that the village was a large one with a small number of prosperous families living there, but Mortham was burned to the ground when the Scots swarmed south after Bannockburn and only the pele tower and a few gravestones survived. Some time later the gravestones were built into the thick buttresses of the gate to the Tudor courtyard. The 15th-century restorations were due to the Rokeby family, who, heedful that border raids were still all too likely, strengthened the tower before they took up residence and enclosed their new courtyard with a defensive wall.

## EGGLESTONE ABBEY: BARNARD CASTLE

In a tranquil setting at Egglestone, on the south bank of the River Tees one mile south-east of Barnard Castle, stand the ruins of the Premonstratensian Abbey of St Mary and St John the Baptist.

**Egglestone Abbey, Barnard Castle.**

Founded in 1196 by Ralph Moulton for an order of Premonstratensian Canons from nearby Easby Abbey, the original community probably consisted only of an Abbot and three canons. Known as White Canons because of the colour of their habits, they lived a life of strict discipline. Throughout its history the abbey suffered financial problems and, in the early 13th century, there was a move to reduce it to the status of a priory. In 1323 it was so severely plundered by the Scots that the canons were sent to other houses of their order until the abbey could be repaired. Following the Dissolution, the site of Egglestone Abbey was sold to Robert Strelley in 1548 and he, in the second half of the 16th century, converted the east wing into an Elizabethan house, now itself a ruin.

## BISHOP AUCKLAND CASTLE

From humble beginnings as a manor house in the late 13th century, when the area was renowned for its good hunting, Auckland Castle became the principal country residence of the Prince Bishops of Durham. The great banqueting hall was converted into a chapel by Bishop Cosin, first Bishop of the Restoration. Named after Bishop Bec, it is reputed to be the largest private chapel in Europe. In

**Bishop Auckland Castle.**

**Deer Shelter, Bishop's Park.**

1647 it passed to Sir Arthur Haslerigg of Naseby, who set about converting it into a great mansion – blowing up part of the chapel in the process! Various Bishops of Durham added to it and Charles I knew it as both a guest and a prisoner.

## DEER SHELTER: BISHOP'S PARK

Bishop's Park, which surrounds the official residence of the Bishop of Durham, extends to 800 acres of mature woodland. In 1767 Bishop Trevor, as part of the landscaping, built a castellated deer enclosure. Gothic in style, it can be found a short distance from the castle. The park is entered from the market place by an imposing lodge and gateway built by Bishop Egerton, and inside the gate a screen wall divides the public park from castle and gardens.

## BINCHESTER ROMAN FORT

In early times Binchester, a quiet little village on the edge of Bishop Auckland, presented an altogether different appearance. Centuries ago, on a flat-topped hill overlooking a bend of the River Wear, the Romans built a fort and called it *Vinovia*, meaning 'water's edge'. A hypocaust, or subterranean heating chamber, was discovered here in the early part of the 19th century when a plough struck a ruined wall. About 200 yards north-west, Dere Street, the main Roman highway, crossed the river on its way from York to Hadrian's Wall. Coins and other relics have been excavated on the site, but the most important discovery was made in May 1891 when a very large altar, in perfect condition, was found in a field south of the fort.

**Binchester Roman Fort.**

## ESCOMB SAXON CHURCH

Nestling at the bottom of a steep bank about a mile and a half west of Bishop Auckland is the village of Escomb. Situated in the middle of this ancient village, in a leafy

**Escomb Saxon Church.**

churchyard enclosed by a circular stone wall, stands one of the most complete Anglo-Saxon churches in England. Small and simple, Escomb Church is built of stones quarried by Roman legionaries and taken from the important Roman settlement at Binchester (*Vinovia*), just over a mile and a half from Escomb on the other side of the Wear. Innumerable stones bear the marks of Roman tooling, or *broaching,* as it is technically called. High up on the exterior of the north wall is a memorial of the sixth legion, which came over to Britain with Hadrian, and was employed by him in making the great central road of Dere Street. The inscription *LEG VI* is upside down. On the south wall, to the right above the porch is a worn Saxon sundial surrounded by a carving of a serpent, with three marks to show the times of services. It is said to be the oldest sundial in England still in its original position. The most striking feature of the interior is the slim, round-headed chancel arch. It has the remains of a fresco on the underside and is said to have been taken intact from one of the Roman buildings at Binchester. Escomb was one of the places mortgaged to the Earl of Northumberland and at the time of the compilation of the *Bolden Book* there were here thirteen villeins, each of whom held an oxgang of land, and rendered similar services to the villeins of North Auckland.

# BRANCEPETH CASTLE

'From every side came noisy swarms

Of peasants in their homely gear;

And, mixed with these, to Brancepeth came

Grave gentry of estate and name,

And captains known for worth in arms,

And prayed the earls in self-defence

To rise, and prove their innocence.'

W. Wordsworth

Situated about five miles south-west of Durham is the picturesque village of Brancepeth. According to an old legend 'a bristled boar of giant size' was slain by Roger de Ferie, and is commonly supposed to have given the name Brancepeth, which is derived from the old 'Brawn's Path'. In the year 1569, on the night of 14 November, the Earl of Northumberland's sleep was rudely interrupted by servants claiming that he was about to be arrested by officers of the Queen. At once he assembled all the men at arms he could muster and made his way to the Neville stronghold at Brancepeth, 'where he found a great number of people' gathered. And so it was, with a tiny force of 1,500 men at arms, under the banners of Charles Neville, 6th Earl of Westmorland and Thomas Percy, 7th Earl of Northumberland,

**Brancepeth Castle.**

they set out from Brancepeth Castle on the ill-fated 'Rising of the North'. When news of this revolt reached the ears of Queen Elizabeth she was incensed: 'the newes unto London came in all the speede that ever might be, and word is brought to our Royale Queene of the rising in the north countrie. Her grace she turned round about, and like a Royall Queen swore, "I will ordayne them such a breakfast as never was seen in the north before". The vast confiscations and forfeitures that followed the suppression of the rebellion produced more changes in the land than any other revolution. The old castle at Brancepeth is said to have been the earliest castellated building in the county, and its foundation is ascribed to the Bulmers, who possessed the estate prior to the Norman Conquest. In 1537, Sir John Bulmer was committed to the Tower of London for playing a leading role in the Pilgrimage of Grace. He was hanged and beheaded at Tyburn on 25 May.

## DOTHEBOYS HALL: BOWES

EDUCATION – At Mr Wackford Squeers Academy, Dotheboys Hall, at the delightful village of Dotheboys, near Greta Bridge. Youth are boarded, clothed, booked, furnished with pocket money, provided with all necessaries, instructed in all languages living and dead, mathematics, orthography, geometry, astronomy, trigonometry, the use of the globes, algebra, single stick (if required), writing, arithmetic, fortification, and every other branch of classical literature.

Terms, twenty guineas per annum. No extras, no vacation, and no diet unparalleled. Mr Squeers is in town, and attends daily, from one till four, at the Saracen's Head, Snow hill.

*Nicholas Nickleby,* Charles Dickens

**Dotheboys Hall, Bowes.**

On 31 January 1838 Charles Dickens arrived by coach at Greta Bridge to collect material for his proposed novel on Yorkshire schools. Dickens had heard grim rumours about the area's boarding schools and also of William Shaw, headmaster of the Shaw Academy. After a short stay in Barnard Castle he went on to the Ancient Unicorn Inn, a well-known coaching inn at Bowes. It was here that Dickens met William Shaw and saw for himself the grim academy at the west end of Bowes. Shaw, the headmaster, had been convicted of negligence in 1823, when some of his pupils went blind from beatings and starvation. In *Nicholas Nickleby* Shaw was stigmatised forever as Whackford Squeers, and the academy, 'where youths are boarded, booked, washed, furnished with pocket-money, provided with all necessaries, for 20 guineas per year', became Dotheboys Hall.

## CROFT BRIDGE

Croft Bridge, which connects the counties of Durham and York, crosses the River Tees four miles south of Darlington. A blue stone on the third arch from the Durham side marks the county boundary. It was here that every new Bishop of Durham was presented with the falchion supposedly used by the Conyers family to dispatch the Sockburn Worm. The custom was for the falchion (a mediaeval broadsword) to be presented to the Bishop of Durham on his first entrance into the diocese by the Lord of Sockburn, who met the Bishop where the river was fordable at Neasham, or if not, on Croft Bridge. Presenting the weapon, he said, 'My Lord Bishop, I here present you with the falchion wherewith the champion Conyers slew the worm, dragon, or fiery flying serpent, which

**Croft Bridge.**

destroyed man, woman and child; in memory of which, the king then reigning gave him the manor of Sockburn, to hold by this tenure, that upon the first entrance of every bishop into the county, this falchion should be presented'.

The Bishop, on taking the falchion into his hand, immediately returned it and wished the Lord of Sockburn long health and enjoyment of his manor. The most recent ceremony took place on 4 July 2003 when the area Dean, the Revd J. Dobson, presented the falchion to the new Bishop of Durham, Dr T. Wright.

On the Durham side the Comet Inn commemorates a well-known bull of the time named Comet, sold for £1,000 guineas by the Collings, breeders of the famous Durham Shorthorns. The bridge was built by Walter Skirlaw, Bishop of Durham in around 1400, as a toll bridge. Tolls ended in 1879.

Croft on Tees is also the place where Charles Lutwidge Dodgson, better known as Lewis Carroll, grew up as a young boy. His father was rector at Croft and the gardens are thought to be the setting for scenes in *Alice in Wonderland*.

## DARLINGTON

'George, thou must think of Darlington; remember it was Darlington sent for thee.' These words were spoken by Edward Pease, a far-sighted Quaker businessman, to George Stephenson, the great locomotive engineer. It was here, on 27 September 1825, that a train of 34 carriages was drawn from Shildon to Darlington and then on to Stockton by *Locomotion No.1*, driven by George Stephenson.

**Darlington.**

This was to become the first passenger railway in the world. Darlington is also the home of the *Northern Echo,* the first halfpenny daily newspaper in England, which began publication in 1869. Outside the library in Crown Street is a memorial to its most famous editor, W.T. Stead, who went down with the *Titanic* in 1912. The centre of Darlington is a wide cobbled market place dominated by the Town Hall clock tower rising above the covered market.

## BRICK TRAIN: DARLINGTON

'This is the Night Mail crossing the border,
Bringing the cheque and the postal order,
Letters for the rich, letters for the poor,
The shop at the corner and the girl next door.
Pulling up Beattock, a steady climb:
The gradient's against her, but she's on time.
Past cotton-grass and moorland boulder
Shovelling white steam over her shoulder,
Snorting noisily as she passes
Silent miles of wind bent grasses.'
 W.H. Auden

**Brick Train, Darlington.**

The North East played a vital role in the development of the railway. By 1890 the North Eastern Railway Company owned a network of lines throughout Durham and Northumberland, their branch lines being a lifeline for the small country towns and villages. In 1994 Darlington Borough Council and Wm Morrison Supermarkets, with additional support from Northern Arts, commissioned the internationally renowned artist David Mach to design a major sculpture for the town of Darlington. At the edge of the A66, on land that was formerly part of the original Darlington–Stockton railway, he was to build a life-size 'Brick Train' sculpture based on the *Mallard* designed by Sir Nigel Gresley. As no two bricks of the construction had a common line, architects used the technology of Computer Aided Design to generate working drawings for the artist. The 'Train' is hollow and home to a colony of Pipistrelle bats, which go in and out through three holes in the side of the sculpture. It is generally agreed that the train looks unusually dramatic when lit up at night.

## HARTLEPOOL HISTORIC QUAY

Few places in the county can boast a longer history than the ancient seaport of Hartlepool. As late as 1614 it was described as the only port town in the county of Durham. In 1967 its merger with West Hartlepool was really a reconciliation, since West Hartlepool was built by Ralph Ward Jackson in the 1830s in protest against coal shipment charges levied by the senior port. In the early 19th century,

**Hartlepool Historic Quay.**

**Ludworth Tower.**

during the Napoleonic wars, according to legend, a French privateer was seen to flounder near the treacherous Longscar Rocks. As the wreckage washed ashore, fishermen found its only survivor, a bedraggled chattering monkey dressed in a military-style uniform. The loyal Hartlepool fishermen subsequently asserted that the creature was a French spy and held a court martial, the punishment being death. A coble's mast with halyard was quickly erected on the Fish Sands and the monkey duly hanged. The award-winning Historic Quay, part of the new marina complex, is a faithful reproduction of an 18th-century seaport, where visitors can experience first-hand what life was like in the times of Lord Nelson. The quay is the current berth of HMS *Trincomalee*, the oldest British warship afloat. Launched in Bombay in 1817, this triple-masted frigate offers a fascinating insight into life aboard a naval warship.

## LUDWORTH TOWER

Ludworth is a typical east Durham mining village. The earliest mention of it is as a property of the priors of Durham. The ruins of Ludworth Tower, one of the few pele towers in Co. Durham, are on the outskirts. It was founded in 1210 by the de Ludworth family as a fortified manor house. Some 200 years later, Thomas Holden enlarged it when Bishop Langley granted him licence to crenellate his manor house. It was later transferred to one Roger Thornton, a merchant, whose daughter married into the Lambton family. Sadly only a few fragments of this building now survive: the barrel-vaulted basement, the three-storey west wall and fragments of the spiral stair in the south wall. The City of Durham now manages the site.

## PIERCEBRIDGE

'It rang an alarm in the dead of the night,
an alarm that for years had been dumb.
And we knew that his spirit was pluming for flight,
that his hour of departure had come.
Still the clock kept the time with a soft and muffled chime,
as we silently stood by its side.
But it stopped, short, never to go again,
When the old man died.'

    Henry Work, 1875

The small village of Piercebridge lies on the River Tees. Although no longer an important site, it was an important river crossing in Roman times and the remains of the bridge built by the Romans can still be seen. It carried the Roman road known as Dere Street, which was the main road north across the river up to Hadrian's Wall. The Romans defended the crossing by building a fort, *Magae*, and as with other crossing sites a civilian settlement sprang up outside the fort. Despite the importance of the crossing it fell out of use once the Romans gave up control in Great Britain. The name of

**Piercebridge.**

Piercebridge, first recorded in 1050, probably means Percy's Bridge and the present bridge at Piercebridge, with its three pointed arches, dates from the early 16th century. At several periods in time records show it was in a state of ruin as a result of damage caused by floods in the river.

The nearby George Hotel, a 16th-century coaching inn, is home to the grandfather clock that inspired Henry Clay Work to write his famous song *My Grandfather's Clock*, from which all long case clocks now take their name. Staying at the hotel in 1875, he was told of the Jenkins brothers who had owned the hotel. The death of the first brother resulted in the malfunction of the floor clock and, at the very moment of the death of the second brother at the age of 90, the clock stopped and never worked again.

Charles Dickens visited Barnard Castle in February 1832 and stayed at the King's Head in the market place, of which he wrote. 'There is good ale at the king's Head. Say you know me and I am sure they will not charge you for it'. While in the town Dickens visited the shop of a clockmaker called Thomas Humphreys where a particular timepiece caught his attention. Enquiring further, he found that the clock had been made by the clockmaker's son, William, who unwittingly provided inspiration for the Dickens novel *Master Humphrey's Clock*.

## ROMALDKIRK

In 1086 the Domesday Book Commissioners had to report, 'There is in Romoldscherce one carucate of land of the geld and there may have been two ploughs. Torfin held it, now Bodin holds it and it is waste…'

**Romaldkirk.**

Set above the River Tees the village of Romaldkirk is one of the prettiest villages in Teesdale. It takes its name from St Rumwald, who built a church there in Anglo-Saxon times. This small group of cottages built around an irregular village green gives the village its beguiling air. The church is cruciform in shape and spans the ages, from the late 12th to the 15th century.

The earliest bye-laws and rulings of the Manor Court from 1630 show that if you allowed your child to throw stones you could be fined 6d, breaking into the pound could cost you 2s 6d, while 'slandering the jury' merited a fine of 6s 8d.

A 'pound', which is a walled enclosure used for stray cattle, can still be seen as you leave the village on the road towards Mickleton.

## SEDGEFIELD: SHROVE TUESDAY

'Tid, Mid, Miseray,
Carling, Palm and Paste Egg Day.'

While for many of us Shrove Tuesday is a day for pancakes, to the residents of Sedgefield it is a day for tradition as the annual Shrove Tuesday game of football kicks off. At 1 o'clock prompt the ball is put through the bullring and the contending factions clash. It is obvious that the use of shin pads is not merely a precaution but a necessity as indiscriminate kicking begins in the ensuing mayhem. Originally contested between the tradesmen and the countrymen, the game has but one aim: to win the ball as

**Sedgefield, Shrove Tuesday.**

in this account of 1884: 'The ball was put through the bull ring in the middle of the village green exactly at 1pm on Tuesday and was then in for play. Both sides were determined to win or die, as it were, and more reckless play we have not witnessed. No rules were adhered to, and scraped shins became the order of the day. After play lasting three hours and fifteen minutes, the tradesmen were declared the victors, they having succeeded in passing the ball over the pond.' It is not clear how old the game is, as records only go back to the 19th century, but claims of 900 years or more should not be dismissed.

Shrovetide is a three-day festival that begins on Shrove Sunday through to Shrove Tuesday. Shrove Tuesday, otherwise known as Pancake Day, is the day before Lent. The word 'Shrove' comes from the custom of Christians confessing, or 'shriving', their sins. Monday is Collop Monday, a collop being an egg fried with bacon, the customary dish eaten that day. The fat from the bacon would then be used to make the pancakes on the following day.

## SEDGEFIELD

Sedgefield has been a market town since the 14th century. Markets were held here every Friday, with cattle fairs being held on the first Friday of April and October. The markets, however, are now almost obsolete, but there is still an agricultural show held at the end of August and the occasional gymkhana. Fox hunting still plays a major part in rural life, while the Sedgefield racecourse continues to hold a number of steeplechase meetings throughout the year.

**Sedgefield.**

Overlooking the town centre on the east side is the 13th-century Church of St Edmund. Robert Rhodes built the tower, crowned with its eight-sided turrets and battlements, as a gift in the 15th century, but sadly, after hundreds of years, the curfew bell no longer tolls every night, although the pancake bell still starts the race on Shrove Tuesday. The font is of particular interest as its base and shaft are made from Frosterly marble and date from the 15th century. Supported by the base and shaft is an intricate bowl of grey Italian marble.

## HARDWICK HALL: SEDGEFIELD

In 1750 John Burdon, the then owner of Hardwick Hall, landscaped the grounds of the hall sited on the mediaeval manor of Herdewyk. The park with its lake, temple of Minerva and follies, is all that is left of a grandiose scheme that ran out of money. The expense of laying out the grounds brought about Burdon's bankruptcy and made it impossible to continue with the mansion that James Paine had designed for him. Durham County Council has now reclaimed the park as a 'country park'.

**Hardwick Hall, Sedgefield.**

Timothy Hackworth Museum, Shildon.

## TIMOTHY HACKWORTH MUSEUM: SHILDON

Before the rise of motoring led to Dr Beeching's railway cuts, Shildon was one of the leading places in the world for the manufacture of railway wagons. The station was probably the oldest in the world. Timothy Hackworth, the pioneering railway engineer, sometimes called the 'father of locomotives', was certainly one of the first in his field and from 1825 was the resident engineer of the Darlington and Stockton Railway, owning his own loco-works. In 1810 Hackworth, working with his friend William Hedley, made locomotives which were known as 'Timothy's Dillies' and 'Puffing Billies'.

Having both been born in Wylam, Timothy Hackworth and George Stephenson were close friends all their lives. Together they co-operated on a number of ventures that included the construction of *Locomotion*, which was built by Hackworth to a design by Stephenson. In 1827 both were adversaries in the famous Rainhill trials. Stephenson was the winner with *Rocket*, while Hackworth's *Sanspareil* was unable to complete the course only because of faulty cylinders – strange as it may seem, Stephenson's son Robert had cast these. There is now a strong belief that the faulty cylinder was used to sabotage *Sanspareil*. While the *Rocket* continued to run for another seven years, the *Sanspareil*, once repaired, was in use for another 30.

A plaque set in the stone monument beside the New Masons Arms recalls one of the greatest days in the history of railways. The inscription reads 'From Shildon near this site the Stockton and Darlington railway Company on the 27th of September, 1825 ran the first passenger train drawn by a steam engine.' These first intrepid passengers had to travel in open coal trucks without protection from the elements or flying sparks from the engine.

## STAINDROP

'Staindrop who from her silver bowers
Salutes proud Raby's battled towers'
*Rokeby*, Sir Walter Scott

The name of the village is said to be a derivative of *Stein Dorf* or *Stein Thorp* meaning stony village. In 1031, following his barefoot pilgrimage from Garmondsway, King Canute gave the small estates of Staindrop in veneration of St Cuthbert as an offering at the shrine of the patron saint of the North.

The history of Staindrop is interwoven with that of Raby and the ill-fated Rising in the North, when in the 16th century 700 barons gathered to plot the overthrow of Elizabeth I in the Baron's Hall. Seven of those who took part were later executed.

On the north side of the village is St Mary's Church. Blocked round-headed windows bear evidence of a church of early Saxon foundation that can be seen in the spandrels of the three eastern arches of the nave.

Among the numerous effigies within is the tomb bearing the figures of Ralph Neville and two wives.

**Staindrop.**

**Raby Castle, Staindrop.**

## RABY CASTLE: STAINDROP

The history of Raby Castle stretches back almost a thousand years to when the estate was owned by King Canute and the mansion was a royal residence, but it was not until the 14th century that the romantic building we see today was begun. In 1378 the Nevilles were granted licence to crenellate Raby for the mighty Neville dynasty. It remained the family stronghold until 1569, the 11th year of the reign of Elizabeth I. On 13 November of that year the 6th Earl of Northumberland, with the intention of replacing Mary, Queen of Scots on the throne, assembled 700 knights in the great Baron's Hall to plot the disastrous 'Rising of the North', an enterprise which brought about the demise of the house of Neville. Defeated, he escaped abroad to lead a beggarly existence and Raby was forfeit to the Crown. In 1621, during the reign of James I, it passed to Sir Henry Vane and has been in the possession of his family ever since. In 1741 the first Lord Barnard was so angered by his son's marriage that he sold the entire contents of the castle, cut down the trees and attempted to destroy the building. The contents have since been recovered. Tradition has it that a hearth-fire has burned in this castle since the time of Edward the Confessor. An underground passage, now blocked off, led from the cellars through to Staindrop Abbey.

## CAULDRON SNOUT: TEESDALE

'Always my boy of wish returns
To those peat-stained deserted burns
That feed the Wear and Tyne and Tees,
And, turning states to strata, sees
How basalt long oppressed broke out
In wild revolt at Cauldron Snout.'
W.H. Auden

From its source on the slopes of Cross Fell, the River Tees flows in an easterly direction until it reaches the North Sea 70 miles away. After descending the numerous cataracts at the head of Teesdale, the river sweeps slowly into Cow Green Reservoir, described by early writers as a ghastly, serpent-like lake. Here, below the dam, it plunges with impetuous force through the rocky gorge of the Whin Sill until finally its peat-stained waters cascade some 200ft down the aptly named Cauldron Snout, England's longest waterfall.

## HIGH FORCE: TEESDALE

From Langdon Beck, the Alston to Barnard Castle road sweeps down with the River Tees past the High Force Hotel. The path winds from the hotel down through the coniferous trees until, on rounding a rock bluff, it comes to a tree-framed waterfall which is the highest in England, falling 70 feet in a single drop. In the 18th century the water flowed in two channels over the dolerite cliff either side of the central rock, but today this only happens after heavy rain. Following the course of the river southerly for a mile and a half, the Whin Sill outcrop churns it once more at Low Force.

Cauldron Snout, Teesdale.

**High Force, Teesdale.**

## MIDDLETON-IN-TEESDALE

Winding, drystone walls hem in the road leading to the small market town of Middleton-in-Teesdale. Once the capital of the dale's lead-mining industry, it is now considered the centre for exploring the wild landscape of Upper Teesdale. In the Horsemarket stands the ornate cast-iron Bainbridge Memorial Fountain, which commemorates the London Lead Company. The company superintendent, Robert Bainbridge, erected it in 1877, with money presented to him on his retirement. Middleton's oldest church, dedicated to St Mary the Virgin, occupies the site of a previous edifice and retains in the nave several mediaeval tombstones which were discovered under the foundations. Just to the north of the church stands the only detached belfry in Durham. Built in Elizabethan times to hold three bells bequeathed by the Reverend William Bele in his will dated 1558, it retains one of its three original bells, which were rung by using both hands and one foot.

**Middleton-in-Teesdale.**

**Willimoteswyke Bastle.**

## WILLIMOTESWYKE BASTLE: BELTINGHAM

Willimoteswyke is a three-storey manor house or bastle at Bardon Mill. The first mention of it is in the 1541 Survey of Border castles and towers. It was noted as belonging to one Nicholas Ridley and having a 'good tower and stone house'. The gatehouse is of the Dunstanburgh type, though on a smaller scale, having a gatehouse and barmkin. The gatehouse, dating from the 16th century, with its tunnel-vaulted carriageway, windows and parapet, is more or less untouched. The earliest parts of the building are from the 14th century while the surrounding walls and windows date from the early 16th century. This is a now a Scheduled Monument and a Grade I listed building protected by law.

## CAUSEY ARCH

Built in 1725 at a cost of £12,000, the remarkable Causey Arch, standing 80ft above the River Causey, is said to be the world's first railway bridge. Constructed of stone, it once carried two railway tracks of timber for the horse-drawn coal wagons. This wagon-way, which was laid down by a group of mine owners known as the Grand Allies, carried coal from Tanfield to the Tyne, and each day 930 horse drawn wagons crossed it in each direction. Every 20 seconds a wagon passed by, with only 50 yards between each one, although this hectic level of use continued for only a short while. By 1738 the nearest pits closed, and in 1740 there was a fire that closed the Tanfield Colliery. By the 1770s the arch had long outlived its usefulness and fell into disuse. Two hundred years later, thanks to the County Engineer, the arch was restored.

**Causey Arch.**

Lumley Castle, Chester-le-Street.

## LUMLEY CASTLE: CHESTER-LE-STREET

It was in 1392 that permission was granted to Ralph, first Baron of Lumley, to fortify his ancestral home near Chester-le-Street. The castle replaced the mediaeval manor house, which stood on the south bank of the River Wear. Visible from the A1, the castle stands four square, with a crenellated tower at each corner. In the centre is a quadrangle, and on the north side is a courtyard surrounded by old out-buildings. The Lumleys can claim their lineage from Ligulf, an Anglo-Saxon nobleman, of whom it is recorded that he was murdered by the chaplain of Walcher, Bishop of Durham. As a result, an angry crowd outside St Mary's Church at Gateshead murdered the Bishop. The first Lord Lumley's dispute with Henry IV caused their lands to be forfeit. The lands were later returned to his son, and the barony to his grandson, but in the reign of Henry VIII they were lost once more, with the beheading of George Lumley on the charge of high treason. In the reigns of Mary and William the barony died out. Richard Lumley, a descendant, later revived it when he came in tenure of the estates.

## CHURCH OF ST MARY & ST CUTHBERT: CHESTER-LE-STREET

The building of the present Church of St Mary and St Cuthbert began in the early 11th century on the site of a small wooden Anglo-Saxon church built in 883 by the monks who fled Lindisfarne with the body of St Cuthbert and settled in Chester-le-Street, seat of nine Saxon bishops. Ethelric, fourth Bishop of Durham (1042–46), replaced this small wooden church with one of stone. Huddled against the north wall of the octagonal belfry tower, dating from about 1409, is an anchorage, a

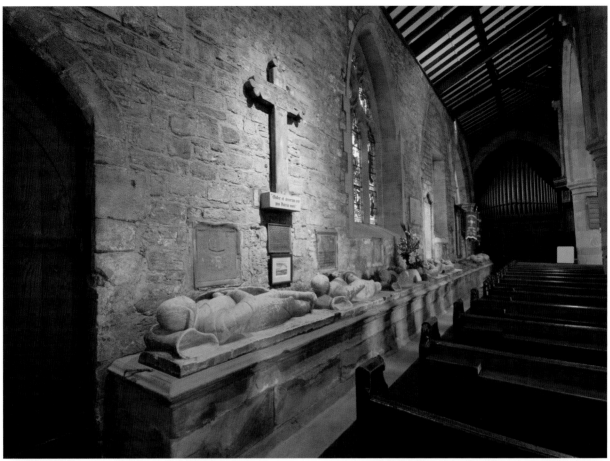

**Church of St Mary & St Cuthbert, Chester-le-Street.**

small cell for an anchorite or hermit who has received permission to lead a religious life within the precincts of a church. An anchorite was under a life vow never to go beyond the boundaries of the church to which he was attached. Sometimes he was a priest, sometimes only a monk. Food was supplied by the faithful, who came to his window for confession, or to consult him as a holy man on any difficulties. A small slit opening into the church allowed the passing through of keys to the church treasury, which the anchorite retained for safekeeping. It is recorded that a certain John Blenkinsopp was permitted to become a hermit at Chester-le-Street at the beginning of the 15th century. Whether he was the original anchorite of this cell is not known, but, bearing in mind that an anchorite's cell did not exist before the Reformation, he was in all probability one of the occupiers of the dwelling. Anchorages were abolished after the Dissolution.

## SHEPHERD & SHEPHERDESS INN: BEAMISH

The Shepherd & Shepherdess Inn at Beamish was built in the 18th century. Above the door are two life-size lead figures of a shepherd and shepherdess, which give the pub its name. The lead figures are said to have been imported from France as 'works of art' when English munitions capability was hampered by a French lead embargo. To bypass this lead embargo works of art in lead were commissioned from abroad, only to be later melted down for munitions. The shepherd and

45

**Shepherd & Shepherdess Inn, Beamish.**

shepherdess were one of 10 such pairs of figures, bought by the squire of Beamish Hall, to be installed on his lawn before they could be melted down. Legend tells us that the squire was returning from a night out when he came across the life-size pair on his lawn. So frightened was he that he immediately gave the figures away to the pub landlord.

## BEAMISH MUSEUM: CHESTER-LE-STREET

Almost all of the novels by Catherine Cookson have been filmed for television here. Voted Museum of the Year in 1986 and European Museum in the year after, Beamish Open Air Museum is the achievement of teamwork between the local authorities of Durham. Opened in 1974, it portrays the social history of the region's daily life at the turn of the century. Steam trains, rattling tramcars, black-leaded kitchen ranges and clove oil in the dentist's surgery all help in bringing it to life. Galvanised tin baths hang in the back yards of a row of pit cottages furnished to show the changing styles throughout the last 100 years.

## TERRIS NOVALIS: CONSETT

On land formerly occupied by Consett Steelworks stands *Terris Novalis,* a stainless steel sculpture by the Turner prize-winning artist Tony Cragg. The monument is one of a series of art works sited along the Coast-to-Coast cycle route known as the C2C. The sculpture, which took four years to realise, was funded through the Arts Council, with contributions from the National Lottery,

**Beamish Museum, Chester-le-Street.**

Terris Novalis, Consett.

Gibside Chapel.

Northern Arts, the Henry Moore Foundation, Derwentside District Council and Consett's Genesis Project. For more than a century the steelworks had a great reputation, but a less well-known fact is that the first Salvation Army band in the world was formed here in 1879.

## GIBSIDE CHAPEL

George Bowes, ancestor of Her Majesty Queen Elizabeth the Queen Mother, laid out the once magnificent Gibside estate. Now the great banqueting house and orangery stare, with their unglazed windows, blindly across Capability Brown's landscaped terraces while Pevsner tells us 'That the buildings of Gibside Estate have been allowed to fall into ruin is a great loss to the county.' The beautifully proportioned chapel, designed in 1760 by James Paine, is built on the lines of a Greek temple. Restored by the National Trust it stands, with its classical portico and four Ionic columns on a balustraded balcony, at the end of a mile-long avenue of trees and was reopened by Queen Elizabeth the Queen Mother on 22 June 1966. A unique three-decker pulpit dominates the interior and elliptical cherry-wood box pews surround the simple central altar. In 1920 some of the fittings from the hall were taken to Glamis Castle.

## BLANCHLAND

In 1165 Walter de Bolbec, a Norman baron, invited 12 White Canons of a Premonstratensian Order known for its great strictness and self-denial to settle on his land by the banks of the River Derwent. Here they built an abbey, naming it after the order's birthplace, Blanche Land in Normandy, from

**Blanchland.**

which the village of Blanchland takes its name. Until the Dissolution of the Monasteries, the abbot was housed in what is now a hotel, the Lord Crewe Arms. In 1623, after being allowed to fall into decline, the estate was purchased from the Radcliffe family by the Forsters of Bamburgh. Towards the end of the 17th century Lord Crewe, Bishop of Durham, married Dorothy Forster, heiress to the estates of Bamburgh and Blanchland, and after paying off the mortgages of the debt-ridden estates he set up a charitable trust to administer them. In the mid-18th century the trustees used stones from the abbey ruins to rebuild the village we see today.

## HARPERLEY POW CAMP: CROOK

Harperley during the war years was a POW Camp. Situated just west of Crook in Weardale, it now boasts ancient monument status, the first World War Two camp to be scheduled. The camp, known as Camp 93, was purpose-built in 1943 to house low-risk POWs. At first the prisoners were housed in tents, but then the first Italians erected huts and by September 1944 a large number of the Italians had been dispersed to farms. This made way for around 900 low-risk German prisoners. The camp initially had around 60 huts, with its own dentist, priest, an extensive library and a large mess hut, in which one of the prisoners painted rural scenes. There was also a theatre with orchestra pit which doubled as a cinema, and prisoners would cheer when Hitler appeared on Pathé newsreels. One of the German prisoners was Bert Trautmann, who became famous as a goalkeeper, playing for

**Harperley POW Camp, Crook.**

Manchester City in the 1956 FA Cup Final. During the game he broke his neck making a spectacular save and, despite being in great pain, played on until the end of the game. A number of prisoners absconded from Harperley; only one was never to be heard of again.

Derwentcote Smelting Mill.

## DERWENTCOTE SMELTING MILL

Derwentcote Smelting Mill, a plain beehive-shaped building situated in the Derwent Valley near Rolands Gill, is the oldest surviving steel-making furnace in Britain. Built in the early 18th century, it produced steel by cementation, a process first recorded in 1601 at Nuremberg, which dominated the steel-making industry until the 19th century. Steel created by this method was known as 'blister steel' because of the blisters covering the steel when it was taken from the furnace. Derwentcote fell into ruins after ceasing operations in about 1870, but restoration commenced in 1987 when it came into the care of English Heritage.

## DILSTON CASTLE

'And when the head that wears the crown
Shall be laid low, like mine,
Some honest hearts may then lament

**Dilston Castle.**

For Radcliffe's fallen line.
Farewell to pleasant Dilston Hall,
My father's ancient seat;
A stranger now must call thee his,
Which gars my heart to greet.'
    *Derwentwater's Farewell*, Robert Surtees

The most wretched figure in all of Northumberland's past is James Radcliffe, the 3rd Earl of Derwentwater. He was born the grandson of Charles II in 1689 and was sent with his cousin James III to be educated at St Germain's. It was for his cousin's cause that the young earl was to lose his life and lands. In 1715, James and his brother Charles joined the Jacobite rising against King George I and both were captured. It was James's Stuart blood and the fact that he was a Roman Catholic that predestined his harsh end. On a cold February morning in 1716 James Radcliffe gave up his life to the headsman on Tower Hill. Only the ruined pele tower remains now of the glories that were once at Dilston. The rectangular tower dates from 15th century and is not named in any of the recognised surveys. The tranquil beauty of the site, combined with the story of the ill-fated earl, ranked as one of the most moving episodes in Northumbrian history, has led over the years to a string of poems and novels. The Radcliffe family succeeded to the manor of Dilston in the early 16th century. This came about through the marriage of Edward

**Durham Castle.**

Radcliffe, a son of Sir Thomas Radcliffe of Derwentwater in Cumberland, to a Dilston heiress, Anne Cartington.

## DURHAM CASTLE

'There are two kings in England, namely the Lord King of England wearing a crown in sign of his regality, and the Lord Bishop of Durham wearing a mitre in place of a crown as a symbol of his regality in the Bishopric of Durham.'

Steward of the Bishopric 1302

Begun in 1072 by William the Conqueror, the original wooden structure of this magnificent Norman castle was, until the mid-19th century, the main seat of the Bishops of Durham. Unique in English history the Prince Bishops ruled the County Palatine, minting their own money, holding their own court, levying taxes and raising their own armies. The oldest part of the castle is the keep, a lofty octagon of irregular sides occupying the summit of an artificial mound, 44ft high, on the north side of the Palace Green. In the 19th century the castle was given over to the University.

## SANCTUARY KNOCKER: DURHAM CATHEDRAL

The English right of sanctuary can be traced back to 597. The distinctive bronze knocker on the broad Norman north door of the cathedral dates back to the 12th century when Bishop Puiset created the north porch. This grotesque head with sightless staring eyes clenches between its jaws the great ring which gave sanctuary to anyone who grasped it throughout the Middle Ages. A fugitive seeking sanctuary within the monastery would, by using the knocker, draw the attention of two monks who kept vigil in a small room above the door. He was then granted the protection of the monastery for a period of 37 days, during which time he would make his confession at St Cuthbert's shrine and swear an oath promising to leave the country within 40 days. Towards the end of the sanctuary period the fugitive was dressed in a black gown with the yellow cross of Saint Cuthbert sewn on to the shoulder and, carrying a rough wooden cross, was escorted to the Bishop's port at Hartlepool. On arrival at the port he was required to embark on the first available ship, regardless of destination. During the reign of Henry VIII an act was passed which required the fugitive to have the letter 'A' branded on the right thumb with a hot iron. In 1624 King James I abolished the right of sanctuary. A sanctuary book records that 331 criminals sought refuge here between 1464 and 1524, most of them for murder.

## DUN COW PANEL: DURHAM CATHEDRAL

After his death in 687 St Cuthbert's body was buried on Lindisfarne (Holy Island) and remained there, undecayed, for 200 years, until, in the ninth century, Danish raiders forced the monks to flee their island, taking the body of St Cuthbert with them. They travelled through the north of England for 120 years, until eventually, in 995, they were told in a vision to take the body to 'Dunholm', the

**Sanctury Knocker, Durham Cathedral.**

Dun Cow Panel, Durham Cathedral.

hill island. They followed a young girl who was looking for her cow and she led them to the rocky peninsular of Durham. On the north-west octagonal tower of the cathedral is a carving of the Dun Cow to commemorate the legend.

## DURHAM CATHEDRAL

'Grey towers of Durham
Yet well I love thy mixed and massive piles
Half church of God, half castle 'gainst the Scot,
And long to roam these venerable aisles
With records stored of deeds long since forgot.'
Sir Walter Scott

Durham Cathedral.

St Cuthbert's Tomb, Durham Cathedral.

The cathedral and castle, around which Durham has grown, stand proudly on a sandstone bluff almost encircled by the River Wear. The best view is from the railway station, where they can be seen in all their grandeur, dominating the ancient city above the steep wooded banks of the river. The cathedral was founded as a shrine for St Cuthbert after marauding Vikings forced the monks to flee from Lindisfarne in 875, taking with them the body of the saint. After wandering throughout the north for 120 years they finally reached Durham. Legend tells of the coffin suddenly becoming rooted to the ground while they were resting and a vision of the saint appeared, telling them of his intention of resting at 'Dunholm'. While discussing how to find this place, the monks overheard a milkmaid tell another that her lost cow was in Dunholm, and by following her they found the island hill. Here they remained for three days, 'having', says Symeon, 'made a little church of the boughs of trees with all speed, wherein they placed the shrine for a time', on the site of the present church of St Mary-le-Bow. By September 998 the first part of the cathedral was built and Cuthbert's coffin was duly transferred to the new building. Durham soon became a place of pilgrimage. In 1237 a tightrope walker employed by the Prior of Durham to entertain the monks fell to his death while walking a rope stretched between the central and west tower of the cathedral. Henry III then wrote to the Prior informing him that the incident had destroyed his hopes of becoming the next Bishop of Durham. Today the castle and cathedral are officially recognised as a World Heritage site.

## ST CUTHBERT'S TOMB: DURHAM CATHEDRAL

'There deep in Durham's gothic shade
His relics are in secret laid,
But none may know the secret place
Save of his holiest servants three,
Deep sworn to secrecy,
Who share that wondrous grace.'
    Sir Walter Scott

Behind the altar, under a marble slab, lie the remains of St Cuthbert, the beloved saint of the north-east. On the night St Aidan died a young border shepherd was keeping watch over his sheep in the Lammermuir hills near Melrose. His companions were all asleep while he held vigil and was saying prayers, when suddenly he had a vision of St Aidan being carried to heaven by angels. The Venerable Bede, in his *Life of St Cuthbert,* wrote, 'And in the morning, learning that Aiden, the bishop of the church at Lindisfarne, a man of specially great virtue, had entered the Kingdom of Heaven at the very time when he had seen him taken from the body, Cuthbert forthwith delivered to their owners the sheep which he was tending, and decided to seek a monastery.' In 1513, after the defeat of the Scottish army at Flodden Field, the banner of the dead Scottish king was hung in triumph over St Cuthbert's shrine in Durham Cathedral. When the monks tried to build a Lady Chapel near Cuthbert's tomb, the saint, who had a long-established fear of them, attributed to a false charge of seduction laid

Galilee Chapel, Durham Cathedral.

against him by the daughter of a Pictish king, is said to have supernaturally interfered with the work and it was abandoned. Later, under the direction of Bishop Pudsey, they built the Galilee Chapel at the west end of the cathedral, away from the shrine.

## GALILEE CHAPEL: DURHAM CATHEDRAL

At the west end of the knave is the Galilee Chapel. In the floor near the font, a few paces from the entrance, is a cross of blue Frosterly marble, which marks the boundary beyond which no woman was permitted to pass in the direction of the shrine of St Cuthbert. Built by Bishop Pudsey in 1170 to accommodate women worshippers denied access to the main body of the cathedral, it is one of the most exquisite examples of Norman masonry in the country. There is much speculation as to the origin of the name. The most commonly accepted is, that when a female relative made an application to see a monk, she was directed to the porch, usually at the western extremity of the church, being answered in the words of Scripture: 'He goeth before you in Galilee, there you shall see him!' It was only here that they were allowed to speak with them. Durham is the only cathedral in England to have a Lady Chapel at the west end instead of the standard position at the east end. Built in 1175, it now houses the resting place of the Venerable Bede.

## ELVET BRIDGE: DURHAM

Elvet Bridge was built in about 1160 by Bishop Hugh Pudsey. It was renovated in 1228 and more extensively repaired in around 1495 under the direction of Bishop Fox. Of the original 14 arches

**Elvet Bridge, Durham.**

**River Banks, Durham.**

recorded by the historian Leyland only 10 are now identifiable. The remaining four are presumably under the road leading to Old Elvet. Two chantry chapels were built on the bridge. The first, dedicated to St Andrew, was built in the latter part of the 13th century at the east end of the bridge, while the second, built at the west end of the bridge, was dedicated to St James in 1312. The House of Correction, built in 1632 beneath the bridge and replacing in part the chapel of St James, can still be clearly recognised at the bottom of the steps leading from the bridge to the riverside.

## RIVER BANKS: DURHAM

Like the crook of a shepherd's staff, the River Wear winds around the city's core. Flowing in from the east it turns sharply south under Elvet Bridge before assuming a northerly direction under Prebends Bridge, leaving the city soon after passing beneath Framwellgate Bridge.

**Durham Big Meeting.**

# DURHAM BIG MEETING

'With bright banners flying and echoes replying
To tuba and trumpet, to fife and drum,
Though yesterday's sorrows weigh less than tomorrow's
Defiant through Durham the pitmen come.'
        Roger Woddis

Sheep now graze in a landscape that once was littered with pitheads and spoil heaps. The demand for coal has gone, the mines have gone, and Durham is becoming green again. It was in October 1992 that the Conservative Government, headed by Margaret Thatcher, delivered the *coup de grâce* to the miners, and a county built on coal, along with its way of life, passed into history. Every July the unity of the miners can be seen at the annual Durham Miners' Gala, when thousands gather for their 'Big Meeting'. In its heyday hundreds of Lodge banners, headed by brass bands, would march in a colourful cavalcade through the narrow streets of Durham to the old racecourse. As they passed through Old Elvet their political leaders would acknowledge them from the balcony of the Royal County Hotel. Today's Gala is a pale imitation of a once proud occasion in the miners' calendar, and old men stare with sadness, remembering times gone by.

# DURHAM LIGHT INFANTRY (DLI) MUSEUM: DURHAM

The original museum opened shortly after World War One at Fenham barracks, Newcastle. It traces the history of the regiment from its beginnings in 1758 to when it was disbanded in 1968. In 1939 the regiment moved to Brancepeth Castle on the outskirts of Durham, where it remained until its closure. In 1969, on the site of the last working mine in Durham City, a new museum was opened to house the DLI collection and Art Gallery.

**Durham Light Infantry Museum, Durham.**

'*Early on the morning of Sunday 5th November, the Companies moved forward to man the front line trench. Every man then looked to the loading of his rifle and the fixing of his bayonet as the zero hour was almost upon us. Chums clasped hands and said "Cheerio" not knowing what the day held in store for them.*'
        Harry Cruddace, 1916

**Durham Regatta.**

## DURHAM REGATTA

With each stroke snapping the boats forward like an arrow from a bow, University boat clubs hiss through the water, tracked by coaches on bicycles along a riverside path. Durham Regatta was founded in 1834, when Durham Original Boat Club competed unsuccessfully against the High Sheriff of the county in a race for six-oared boats. More races were to follow that day, and the event, held to commemorate the Battle of Waterloo, climaxed with a firework display in the evening. So began a regatta which is the second oldest in the England.

## FINCHALE PRIORY; DURHAM

Finchale Priory, the picturesque ruins that lie three miles downstream from Durham in a loop of the River Wear, had one of the most unusual origins in monastic history. The story begins with St Godric who, at the age of 20, turned from the life of a peddler to that of a seafarer. He was probably the 'Guderic, a pirate from the Kingdom of England', who, while in the Holy Land in 1102, once allowed the King of Jerusalem to travel in his vessel. On returning to England some two years later, after making a pilgrimage to the shrine of St James of Compostella in Spain, he resolved to leave all worldly affairs behind and start life anew as a hermit. Between 1104 and 1106 he joined a hermit at Walsingham, where he was told in a vision that St Cuthbert would find a place for him at Finchale. On the death of his companion, Godric left for Durham to discover the location of his promised

Finchale Priory, Durham.

retreat. In 1110 Ranulf Flambard, Bishop of Durham, gave him permission to settle at Finchale. For the first five years he lived about a mile upstream from the present ruins, but in 1115 he moved south, and in a short time had built himself a turf-covered dwelling-place, with a little chapel of timber attached which he dedicated to St Mary. He continued to live here until 1170, when he died at the patriarchal age of 105, and his hermitage came into the hands of Durham Cathedral. In 1237 work started on the permanent buildings, the ruins of which are now visible, but sometime during the 14th century it became a retreat hostel for the monks of Durham, who, by using a rota system, would spend three weeks there each year resting. This arrangement continued until the Dissolution.

## CHERRYBURN HOUSE: STOCKSFIELD

'Cherryburn House, the place of my nativity, and which for many years my eyes beheld with cherished delight, is situated on the south side of the Tyne, in the county of Northumberland, a short distance from the river. It was with infinite pleasure that I long beheld the beautiful wild scenery which was there exhibited.'

*A Memoir of Thomas Bewick*, 1828

Thomas Bewick, famous for his amazing woodcuts of British birds, was born at Cherryburn in 1753. At the age of 14 he was apprenticed to Ralph Beilby for a £20 apprentice fee. One of his first

**Cherryburn House, Stockfields.**

jobs was blocking-out on wood and etching sword blades. His work represents a zenith in the art of the engraver, and the farmhouse where he was born now houses an exhibition of his life and works.

## FEATHERSTONE CASTLE

'Hoot awa' lads, hoot awa'.
Hae ye heard how the Ridleys and Thirwalls and a',
Ha' set upon Albany Featherstonehaugh,
And taken his life at the Deadmanshaugh?'
*Marmion*, Sir Walter Scott

Featherstone is one of the most striking castles in Northumbria. There was a 'hall' house at Featherstonehaugh in the 14th century when Thomas de Featherstonehaugh built a tower with a vaulted basement. In the 16th century Richard Featherstonehaugh became chaplain to Catherine of Aragon and, because of his loyalty to Henry VIII's first wife, was executed. In mediaeval times the family were involved in border raids and local feuds, including an affray with the Ridleys, and the death of Sir Albany Featherstonehaugh in 1530 was the result of these feuds. To this day the site of this murder is known as Deadman's Haugh, which lies about a mile from the castle across the river.

**Featherstone Castle.**

The castle, like many others in Northumberland, has a ghost or ghosts. The story runs that in an old house at Hardriding lived a certain Hugh Ridley, who was in love with the heiress of Featherstone. The heiress's father, however, had other ideas about a bridegroom for his daughter, and the girl was married, to her horror, to a distant cousin.

Following the ceremony, the guests and bride set out on a hunt in the nearby woods. However, they were ambushed by the heiress's lover and his friends, and the whole party was killed. In the confusion of the mêlée the bride too was slain and, overcome with grief, the lover killed himself. In the meantime, the bridal breakfast had been prepared as the baron awaited the return of his guests. It was not until midnight that the door opened and in staggered a bloodstained bridegroom and guests, taking their seats in silence. To his horror the baron realised that these were ghosts, and as he felt a cold blast sweep across the hall the bridal party faded away. It is said that every year at the same time of day the ghostly bridal party may be seen riding in the castle woods. The verse at the beginning of this piece was attributed to Scott, although Surtees was actually the man who wrote it!

## ANGEL OF THE NORTH: GATESHEAD

At the edge of the A1, on land that was formerly occupied by the pithead baths of Teams colliery, stands Britain's largest sculpture, the awe-inspiring *Angel of the North*. Seen by 90,000 motorists each day, this impressive 65ft high giant, with outspread arms, gazes silently southward on the outskirts of Gateshead. Weighing 200 tonnes, it has the 175ft wingspan of a jumbo jet. Commissioned in 1994 by

**Angel of the North, Gateshead.**

Gateshead Council, the Angel was designed by internationally renowned sculptor Antony Gormley. When erected in 1998 it was given worldwide publicity and became the toast of the arts world after winning the prestigious South Bank Show Award for Visual Arts in 1999. Its silhouette, on a hill top site at the head of the Team Valley, has become a new landmark in the area.

## MILLENNIUM BRIDGE: GATESHEAD

Linking the Gateshead Quays to the Newcastle Quays, the world's first and only tilting bridge opens to allow ships to pass beneath its graceful arch. Designed by the combined efforts of Wilkinson and Eyre Architects and Gifford Brown Partners, the Millennium Bridge is last of the distinguished bridges that cross the Tyne. In the last weeks of November of the Millennium year the bridge made its six-mile journey up the river from Wallsend to the Baltic Quays area. At a weight of more than 800 tonnes and carried by Europe's largest floating crane, *Asian Hercules*, it was slowly lowered into place. The leader of Gateshead Council, Mick Henry, said: 'when we chose the design for the Gateshead Millennium Bridge we knew we had something very special. The many awards and accolades it has received for its design and construction have certainly proved us right'. In 2007 the Gateshead Millennium Bridge appeared on a new pound coin from the Royal Mint.

**Millennium Bridge, Gateshead.**

The Sage, Gateshead.

## THE SAGE: GATESHEAD

The Sage music centre opened on 17 December 2004 and is the region's latest home for music. This £70 million project, designed after consulting with audiences, has helped establish Tyneside's position in the music world and acts as a base for the Northern Sinfonia. The Sage provides three auditoriums and music facilities for people of all ages. Sir Norman Foster designed this dramatic glass and stainless steel building on the south quayside. The roof of the breathtaking building, made up of over 3,500 square metres of glass, allows light to flood the building during the day. A glazed concourse around the front and sides provides stunning views of the quayside.

## BALTIC CENTRE: GATESHEAD

Gateshead, once dismissed by J.B. Priestley as a town that appeared 'to have been invented by an enemy of the human race', decided in the early 1990s that culture and the arts provided the key to a regeneration strategy. For more than half a century the huge silo of the Baltic flour mill has presided over the riverside there. Built in the 1950s for Joseph Rank Ltd for holding grain for flour, it became redundant by the 1980s. An imaginative scheme in 2002 saw the silo rise like a phoenix from the ashes to form part of the quays project. Now restored, it competes with venues in Paris and New York as an international arts centre.

**Baltic Centre, Gateshead.**

**Hexham Manor Office.**

# HEXHAM MANOR OFFICE

The ancient market town of Hexham in the fertile Tynedale valley was once a frequent target of Scottish raiders because, like many of England's border towns, it was not walled. The Manor Office takes its name from its having been used for the transaction of business with the manor of Hexham. Originally built as a gaol in 1332 by the Archbishop of York, it was the first building in England to be specially built for this purpose and was used as such until 1824. The first gaoler was a local barber, John de Cawode, who was paid twopence a day to look after the prisoners. Many a bold Northerner has languished in this jail awaiting execution. On one occasion, shortly after Queen Elizabeth's succession, the jailer found himself so much in sympathy with his prisoners that he not only released them, but also went with them. Today it houses the Border History Museum and Tourist Information Centre.

## ALLENDALE BA'AL FESTIVAL

Set in England's high Pennines, the town of Allendale has the distinction of being the geographical centre of Great Britain. In reference to this claim a sundial on the south wall of the unassuming Church of St Cuthbert bears the town's latitude and longitude. In 1715 Robert Patten, one of the curates of this church, was chaplain to General Forster during the Jacobite rebellion. After the surrender, and at the expense of his friends, he turned King's Evidence to save his own life. The Ba'al Fire Ceremony, a pagan celebration for the winter solstice, is still kept on New Year's Eve. As the midnight hour approaches, 40 guisers with blackened faces parade through the streets carrying blazing tar barrels on their heads. The guisers, some of whom have held the right to carry the flaming barrels for more than half a century, had this honour passed on to them from their fathers. A huge bonfire is lit in the market place and the tar barrels are thrown upon it to the chant 'Be damned to he who throws last'. Then the townsfolk and guisers dance until midnight, when the 'first footing' begins. Without documentary evidence as to the roots of this ancient festival, local folklore suggests it is Viking in origin and deeply rooted in the fire worship of pagans.

**Allendale Ba'al Festival.**

**Hexham.**

# HEXHAM

'Away with the parson's shilling
and away with the cap and feather,
I want to see my lass who lives in Hexhamshire.'
*The Hexhamshire Lass*

The 1,300-year-old market town of Hexham was in the past known as Haguststaldham, derived from the old English word Hago-steald, a 'young warrior', but it was from St Wilfrid that it derived its episcopal pride. In the year 674 he was in favour at the court of Egfrid, when Queen Etheldreda gave him land, which formed part of her dowry, in order that he might found a bishopric. Wilfrid, who at the time was Archbishop of York, then appears to have behaved in a most unholy manner by persuading Etheldreda to leave her husband and take the veil. In 681, at a time when Wilfrid was once more in disgrace and a fugitive in Rome, it was decided to divide Bernicia into two bishoprics; those of Lindisfarne and Hexham. Prior to this Bernicia, stretching from the Tees to the Firth of Forth, had constituted a single See.

The abbey suffered many attacks by marauding Danes and Scots, who appeared to have a strong liking for setting fire to it, but despite its problems the abbey has gradually developed into the

77

majestic building we see today. Its treasures include the finest Anglo-Saxon crypt in England and the stone 'Saint Wilfrid's Chair' that was once used as a sanctuary stool and is reputed to be the coronation seat for the Kings of Northumbria. Rich mediaeval furnishings fill the chair, including rare painted panels and 38 misericords, the backs of which were sold for firewood during the 19th century.

The area to the south of the town is still known as Hexhamshire. It was, until Queen Elizabeth I annexed it back, a separate county, and by the 17th century it was one of the country's leading leatherwork centres, specialising in gloves. It was at one time producing nearly 900,000 pairs of 'Hexham tan' gloves a year.

## JARROW PRIORY

With the erection of the monastery of St Paul in 681, on the site of a long-deserted Roman fort, St Benedict Biscop and his friend Ceolfrid founded one of the most ancient and famous of all English monasteries. Dedicated on 23 April 685, the first monks for this monastery were transferred from Monkwearmouth, with which it was consolidated, and the united churches became the monastery of St Peter and St Paul. The Venerable Bede entered the Jarrow monastery when he was about seven years of age and remained there, with occasional visits to the sister house, until his death in 735. During their attacks on the Northumbrian kingdom it was sacked twice by the Danes, once in 794 and again in 866. In 1083 Bishop Carileph removed the monks both from Jarrow and Wearmouth to Durham, and in Jarrow reduced both houses to cells under the monastery of St Cuthbert. At the Dissolution of the religious houses by Henry VIII, the cell at Jarrow was, according to Speed's account, valued at £40 7s 8d per annum. It was at Jarrow, in 731, that Bede wrote his famous and monumental *Ecclesiastical History of the English People*, and he also made the first translation of St John's Gospel into English.

## LANGLEY CASTLE

Overlooking the fertile valley of the South Tyne, midway between Hexham and Haltwistle, stands perhaps the best example of a tower house in Northumberland – the beautiful square tower of Langley Castle. First mentioned in 1365, it was later to become the property of the Earl of Northumberland. By 1541 it was already in ruins, and the once great stronghold of the de Lucys, owned by almost all the great Northumbrian families at one time or another, was gone. Sir Robert Bowes reported in 1550, 'for the most parte the fortresses, towers and piles upon the utter side or frontier of those east marches have been in tymes past rased and casten downe by the Scottes and yet be not repaired which is muche pitty to see'. Ruined and neglected, it seemed that Langley had died, until that is, Mr C.J. Bates, the Northumbrian historian, bought the estate in 1882 and restored it to its former glory. In the lawless days of marauding Scots the bells of Langley would ring out to warn the people of approaching danger. Prior to becoming a hotel the castle was a private girls' school, whose headmistress was a Miss Hebron.

**Jarrow Priory.**

**Langley Castle.**

## MONKWEARMOUTH PRIORY

It is 1,326 years since 'the pious servant of Christ', Benedict Biscop, began to build a monastery in honour of the most blessed Peter, the chief of the Apostles, on the north side of the mouth of the Wear. The venerable and devoted King of Northumbria, Egfrid, gave him a site and helped him in the work. That is what Bede tells us. 'Benedict', as Bede further states, 'went to France and procured stone masons who could build him a church of stone in the style of the Romans, which he greatly admired'. Benedict was a Northumbrian nobleman who, after serving at the court of the Northumbrian king, entered the monastery at Lerins near Cannes, making several pilgrimages to Rome. He returned to England in 669 with Theodore of Tarsus, Archbishop of Canterbury, to promote Christianity in his own land. It was the books he brought back from his travels that enabled Bede,

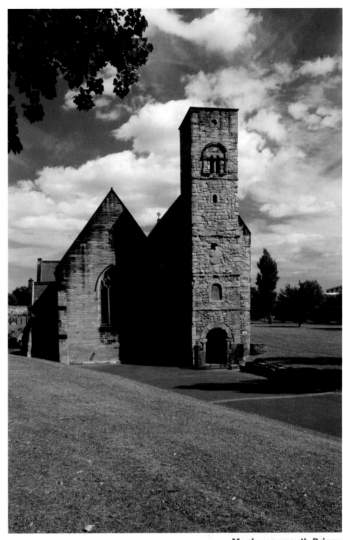

Monkwearmouth Priory.

who had entered Monkwearmouth as a novice, to continue his studies before moving to Jarrow. Within a year of laying the foundations the roof was on and masses were celebrated. St Peter's was the first English church to use glass in its windows.

## PENSHAW MONUMENT

Crowning the smooth, steep, green slopes of Penshaw Hill, a replica of a Grecian temple marks the place where the Lambton worm 'lapped his tail'. It was erected in 1844 in memory of John Lambton, Earl of Durham, to commemorate services he had rendered to his country. Penshaw Hill was chosen as the site because for many years it had been connected with the property of the Lambton family. Although the design of the monument is copied from the Temple of Theseus, the dimensions are exactly double the original. The columns of the Temple of Theseus are 3ft 3in, while those of the Durham memorial are 6ft 6in. One of the columns has a staircase in it, though access has been closed for several years. So commanding and conspicuous is its position that it can be seen from almost all parts of the district.

**Penshaw Monument.**

## PRUDHOE CASTLE

Prudhoe Castle, perched on a prominent spur overlooking the River Tyne, was built in about 1165 by Odinel de Umfraville, on the site of an earlier stronghold of earth and wood. The first Umfraville in England was Robin with the Beard, William the Conqueror's right-hand knight who, for his services, was given the liberty of Redesdale to defend, with the aid of the sword worn by William himself. Later the huge barony of Prudhoe was added to the Umfraville possessions. In 1173 William the Lion of Scotland swore to destroy the castle and laid siege to it, but he gave up the attempt after only three days and was captured shortly afterwards when trying to take Alnwick. In frustration his followers spoilt the gardens and cornfields outside the castle walls and stripped the bark off the orchard apple trees. The impressive keep, with its tall turret rising above the rest of the castle, is one of the smallest Norman rectangular keeps in England. The Inner Barbican adjoins the Gatehouse, which was without any portcullis but had iron lattice gates at each end of its passageway.

It was near here, on Monday 28 January 1766, that a certain William Fenwick and friends were foxhunting. After some hours of chase the fox ran for safety into the nearby drift of a coal mine, followed by the hounds. In darkness and hot pursuit they followed for nearly an hour. Finally they caught and killed the fox before it could reach daylight and escape.

Prudhoe Castle.

# ARBIEA: SOUTH SHIELDS

In Roman times South Shields was called Tunnocelum, and the Tyne was a very important river, for at its mouth was the starting point of the famous Tenth Iter of Antonine, one of the great marching

Arbiea, South Shields.

83

routes of the army. The strongly fortified Roman fort of Arbeia was therefore not only an important fortress, but also a great trading centre. The Fifth Cohort of Gauls, who have left numerous memorials of their occupation, garrisoned it. While digging the foundations of an extension to Baring Street Board School, workmen uncovered a slab of stone with an inscription to commemorate the construction of waterworks to supply the fortress. The inscription reads: 'The Emperor Caesar, Grandson of the divine Severus, Son of the Divine Antoninus the great, Marcus Aurelius Severus Alexander, Benevolent, Prosperous, August, Chief Priest, Endowed with the Tribunitial Power, Father of his Country, The Consul, has brought Water into the Fortress for the use of the soldiers of the Fifth Cohort of the Gauls, Marius Valerianus, His Lieutenant, Propraetor, directing the Works.'

## *TYNE* LIFEBOAT: SOUTH SHIELDS

'Man the lifeboat, man the lifeboat
Help! Or yon ship is lost;
Man the lifeboat, man the lifeboat
See how she's tempest toss'd.'

*Tyne* lifeboat, South Shields.

'Ah see! The crew are struggling now
Amidst the billows' roar;
They're in the boat! They're all afloat!
Hurrah! They've gained the shore.
Bless the lifeboat, bless the lifeboat!
Oh! God, thou'lt hear our prayer.
Bless the lifeboat, bless the lifeboat!
No longer we'll despair.'

South Shields has the honour of being the birthplace of the lifeboat, which was invented here in 1789. That year witnessed many disastrous wrecks along the coast near South Shields. In the month of September a ship named the *Adventure* was wrecked on the Herd Sand in full view of thousands of spectators, but because of the atrocious weather conditions no assistance could be given to the unfortunate crew. These continuous disasters had the effect of raising public feelings and it was decided to set about providing an effective way to give assistance to ships in distress. A public meeting was held and funds raised to pay for the best model of a boat for life-saving purposes. The idea of building a self-righting boat came from William Wouldhave, a painter from South Shields, who, while studying a wooden spoon, noticed that when divided the two parts would always float with the points upwards, whichever way they were thrown into the water. It is on this principle that the modern lifeboat of today is based.

## SUNDERLAND LUSTREWARE

Many years ago, when oil lamps and candles lit rooms, people loved to have things around them that shone and glowed in this soft light. Wealthy people had their silverware and glass, but the less well-off had to do it in other ways. One of these was having lustred pottery and china on the mantelpieces, reflecting back the light from the fire. Sunderland began to make its famous lustreware from the early part of the 18th century and the varieties of lustre are many, including jugs, mugs and other items. The rims around these 'Sunderland' items are painted with a mottled sort of purple-pink lustre, and this effect is arrived at by blowing oil on to the painting through a pipe using gauze. The pottery, often adorned with a commemorative verse or inscription, also carried transfers of ships in full sail or a picture of Sunderland's Wearmouth Bridge.

**Sunderland Lustreware.**

Hylton Castle, Sunderland.

# HYLTON CASTLE: SUNDERLAND

For more than six centuries Hylton Castle was the home of one of the oldest, richest and most powerful families in the county of Durham. This great and ancient family at one time possessed not only the manor of Hylton, but also others in Durham, York and Northumberland. War seems to have been the pleasure of the Hyltons: one was killed in Kent, one in Normanby, one in France, three in the Holy Wars, one at Agincourt, three at the Battle of Bordeaux, five at Market Bosworth and four at Flodden Field. Over the years a total of 21 deaths in battle are recorded.

Hylton Castle has long had the reputation of being haunted by a barguest or local spirit identified with the death of an unfortunate servant killed by one of the barons of Hylton. The baron had ordered his horse, and being impatient went to the stable and found the boy asleep, whereupon he struck what proved to be a deathly blow with a scythe. He then covered the body of his victim with straw and at night threw it into the pond, where the skeleton was discovered.

The ballad of *The Cau'd lad of Hylton* tells how the murdered youth, Roger Skelton, used to pace round the castle hall with his head literally in his hand, singing, 'soft and low':

'Hylton's line dishonoured fall;
Lay with the dust proud Hylton's walls,
Murder blots the household sword;
Strip the lands from Hylton's lord.'

Perhaps this story originated from the recorded coroner's inquest held on 3 July 1609 on the body of Roger Skelton. Hylton obtained a free pardon on 6 September 1609.

**Washington Coat of Arms, Hylton.**

## WASHINGTON COAT OF ARMS: HYLTON

Once noted for its pottery, lustre and enamel ware, the village of North Hylton, situated on the north bank of the River Wear, is perhaps better known for the forlorn ruins of a castle gatehouse painted by Turner. Carved in the stonework of the turret battlements are many shields of arms; among them is one bearing the Washington coat of arms, three stars and two bars. This shield, some 500 years old, is the oldest known stone carving of the Washington arms and was later adapted by George Washington for the American Stars and Stripes.

## SOUTER LIGHTHOUSE: WHITBURN

Worn by the ceaseless action of the sea, the huge limestone cliffs that fringe the shore south of Marsden Bay have become a variety of bays, coves and inlets. Detached rocks of every imaginable shape and size add to the scenic confusion of natural arches, isolated pillars and caves, around which the waters churn. In 1869 over 20 vessels came to grief on the hazardous reefs off the Durham coast and in consequence the Elder Brethren of Trinity House London decided to build a new electric light and fog-signal station at Souter Point. Opened in January 1871 at a cost of £15,148, Souter Lighthouse (pronounced Sooter) was the first shore-based lighthouse to be powered by electric alternators using a principle adopted by Sir James N. Douglass, chief engineer to Trinity House. It was a remarkable piece of optical skill that provided a light equal to 800,000 candles. In addition to the intense brilliance, Souter's foghorns were so powerful that the keepers were paid an additional twopence an hour as 'noise money'. The lighthouse ceased operating in 1988 when it became an automatic radio beacon. It is now in the care of the National Trust.

**Souter Lighthouse, Whitburn.**

**Washington Old Hall.**

# WASHINGTON OLD HALL

It was in 1173 that William de Hertburn exchanged his manor with Hugh de Puiset, Bishop of Durham, for that of Wessynton at a rent of £4 a year and assumed the local name of William de Wessynton, which is recorded in Durham charters. Washington Old Hall, built by the Wessynton family in 1183, is the ancestral home of George Washington, America's first President, a direct descendent of Walter de Wessynton who lived in the 14th century. Wessynton is the Anglo-Saxon spelling of Washington, who were lords of the manor. The family remained here until 1367 when the manor was sold and they moved to Sulgrave in Northamptonshire. Their coat of arms – three stars and two stripes – was the origin of *Old Glory*, the American flag. The deed of sale, with its wax seal bearing the three stars and two stripes, is preserved in Durham Cathedral Library. A Washington village girl, born in 1868, also grew up to earn distinction. Gertrude Bell was one of the most extraordinary women of her times, achieving feats considered impossible by the opposite sex. She set out from Damascus in 1913 to Hail, some 500 miles across the desert. There the local tribesmen forbade her to travel further south and so, turning north, she then rode a further 500 miles to Baghdad. It was, and still is, considered one of the greatest journeys ever undertaken by a lone woman explorer.

**Weardale, Killhope Wheel.**

# WEARDALE: KILLHOPE WHEEL

'My father was a miner, he lived down in the town,
'Twas hard work and poverty that always kept him down.
He aimed for us to go to school, but brass he couldn't pay,
So we had to go to the washing rake for fourpence a day'.

Situated in the remote windswept landscape of upper Weardale stands the remains of Park Level
Lead Mine at Killhope. It opened in 1853 on land leased from the Bishop of Durham by the Blackett-
Beaumont Company, whose interest in lead mining dated back to the late 17th century. However,
by 1883 the industry had sunk into decline and it was taken over by the London Lead Company,
which extensively mined the Derwent, Teesdale and Weardale valleys and was the first company to
introduce the five-day week. The mine closed in 1916 and the neglected site fell into decay. In the
1970s Durham County Council began minor repairs to the derelict buildings before restoring the
crushing mill, powered by the 33ft diameter by 6ft wide waterwheel, which was fed from two small
hillside reservoirs. It was opened as a Visitors' Centre in 1984 and is now thought to be the best
preserved lead-mining site in Britain.

# RIVER TYNE TO RIVER COQUET

**Aydon Castle.**

## AYDON CASTLE

A wealthy merchant named Robert de Raymes originally built Aydon Castle as a private residence at the end of the 13th century. Situated in a commanding position above the deep wooded ravine of Cor Burn, just north of Corbridge, it is one of the finest fortified manor houses in England. The licence to crenellate was obtained in 1305 after Edward I illegally assumed the Scottish throne and the need for defence became obvious because of the increasing border lawlessness. In 1315 Raymes wrote that he had 'lately fortified his dwelling at Aydon with a wall of stone and lime against the king's enemy, the Scots', and left the castle in the care of Hugh de Gales. At the approach of the Scottish army this unchivalrous custodian proceeded to 'conspire with the Scots', inviting them to plunder and burn the castle. In the 17th century the castle became a farmhouse and remained in private ownership until 1975, which helped to retain its notable features.

**Black Middens Bastle, Bellingham.**

## BLACK MIDDENS BASTLE: BELLINGHAM

'If any Englishman steal in Scotland, or any Scotsman steal in England, any goods or cattels amounting to 12d, he shall be punished by death.'

Border Commissioners, 1605

On either side of the border the inhabitants belonged to a clan or family and if any member were in trouble they would come to his assistance. In 1296 Edward I appointed the first Warden of the English Marches to control law and order in the region. From the mid-16th century, in response to border raids by the Reivers, wealthy farmers built a variant on the pele tower known as a bastle house. These two-storey fortified farmhouses tend to be found in the more remote areas of the Border country.

In times of danger, when Reivers might be around, stock would be barred in at the ground floor, while the family accessed the upper floor via a ladder, which would be drawn up behind them.

At an isolated spot in North Tynedale sits Black Middens bastle house.

## BELLINGHAM: 'THE LANG PACK'

The body of Saint Cuthbert is supposed to have rested here on its long journey from Lindisfarne to Durham and people still like to draw water from the well named after him. The well, the water from which is still being used in the church, is supposed to have the power of healing. Saint Cuthbert's

Bellingham, The Lang Pack.

Church has a unique stone roof, well restored in recent years. In the 18th century, to counteract the force of the barrel-vaulted stone roof, buttressing was carried out. These stone slabs were laid after two fires had destroyed the previous roof.

There is a curiously pack-shaped tombstone to mark a 700-year-old grave in the churchyard. Known locally as 'the Lang Pack', it tells the curious tale of a peddler who called one day at Lee House and asked for lodgings. The master was away from home so the maid refused his request. But she did allow the man to leave his heavy pack in the kitchen. Some time later she saw the pack move and called for help from a ploughboy. On firing into the sack he saw blood pouring out, and inside lay the body of a young man. The servants, realising a raid was impending, called for help and then blew the silver horn they found on the body. The robbers, when they came, were met by force and fled.

Outside Bellingham's town hall sits a Chinese gun, captured at Fort Taku during the Boxer Rebellion in China in 1900.

## HESLEYSIDE: THE CHARLTON SPUR

'Over the Borderland, wha' will gan wi' us,
Saddle your horses an' buckle your blades,
We will bring back wi' us fat Scottish cattle,
Good Scottish horses and fair Scottish maids.'
C.F. Palmer

In a report to Queen Elizabeth I, Sir Robert Bowes wrote, 'The countreye of North Tynedaill which is more plenished with wild and misdemeaned people, may make of men on horsebak and upon foote about six hundred. They stand most by fower surnames, wherof the Charlton's be the chiefe.'

Nothing now remains of the Charlton family stronghold. The pele tower that once stood at Hesleyside was garrisoned

**Hesleyside, the Charlton Spur.**

by 50 men and had a mansion attached to it on the east side, but it was demolished and the mansion turned into a country house.

The present house now seems to have forgotten its turbulent past. In reiving days, when supplies were low, the lady of the house suggested, by means of a spur carried on a dish, that it was time to ride out and 'lift' some of their neighbours' cattle. The men would need no encouragement, and the lady of Hesleyside could be sure that her larder would soon be well stocked with Scottish beef and mutton.

A painting by Bell Scott at Wallington Hall, *The Spur*, is a reminder of these wild times. *The Spur* is currently in the care of the trustees of Bellingham Heritage Centre and is on show throughout the season.

## BELSAY HALL CASTLE

At Belsay we can see at once the transition from castle to mansion house. It was built in the time of Edward III by John de Middleton and extended by the addition of a manor house in 1614. In the 19th century Sir Charles Monck built Belsay Hall to his own design, from plans drawn up by the young architect John Dobson. Sir Charles, a lover of Grecian architecture, brought workmen from Greece to build his new home. The honey-coloured sandstone with which the mansion is built was quarried from the grounds at the back. In the second half of the 19th century Arthur, Sir Charles's grandson, finished landscaping the garden, which soften the severity of the house. In the 14th century the family were temporarily evicted from the castle when Sir Gilbert Middleton quarrelled with the Crown and held two cardinals and the bishop elect of Durham to ransom. It was only when an ancestor married the daughter of Sir John de Striveling that it was recovered. To this day it remains in the hands of the same family.

**Belsay Hall Castle.**

**Cambo.**

## CAMBO

In 1740 Sir Walter Blackett began to replace the mediaeval village of Camhoe, sited on a ridge above Wallington Hall, with the model estate village of Cambo. Its oldest building is the Post Office, a former 16th-century bastle house. In the centre of the village is the Dolphin fountain, built by Sir Charles Edward Trevelyan as part of the remodelling. In 1911 Sir George Otto Trevelyan converted the old schoolhouse, which Capability Brown had attended as a child, into the village hall.

## CHESTERS: FORT & BATH HOUSE

'Octavius to his brother Candidus, greetings. The hundred pounds of sinew from Marinus I will settle up. From the time when you wrote about this matter, he has not even mentioned it to me. I have several times written to you that I have bought about five thousand mondii of ears of grain, on account of which I need cash. Unless you send me some cash, at least five hundred denarii, the result will be that I shall lose what I have laid out as a deposit, about three hundred denarii, and I shall become embarrassed. So I ask you send me some cash as soon as possible. The hides which you write about are still at Cataractonium, write that they be given to me and the wagon about which you write. And write to me what is with that wagon. I would have already been to collect them except that I do not care to injure the animals while the roads are bad.'

Letter: Octavius to Candidus

**Chesters, Fort & Bath House.**

The Roman fort on Hadrian's Wall at Chesters marks the point of the first major obstacle on its route from east to west. So that the wall could continue down to the water's edge, a number of timber bridges and stone piers were built to cross the river. The name of Chesters is first mentioned in the late fourth century where it is listed as *Cilurnum* in the Notitia Dignitatum. *Cilurnum*, which we now know as Chesters, was built to house cavalry that were capable of rapid strikes into the 'barbaric' north. As is usual for all cavalry forts on the wall, it was built on the line of the barrier, with three of its gateways opening to the north side. The Roman bathhouse at Chesters has been acclaimed as the most impressive on the wall, and is one of the best-preserved examples in all the Roman Empire. It was built for the soldiers stationed at the fort, close to where the bridge crossed the river.

## CORBRIDGE: VICAR'S PELE

On the north bank of the Tyne, 17 miles west of Newcastle, is the attractive mediaeval market town of Corbridge. In 1830 Hodgson had this to say. 'The town (for such its antiquity demands that it be styled) is dirty, and in all the streets except which the Newcastle and Carlisle road passes, is filthy with middens and pigsties, with railing before them of split boards etc. The population seems half-fed; the women sallow, thin-armed, and the men flabby, pot-bellied and tender-footed; but still the place bears the appearance of being ancient'. Occupying the site of a monastery of 771, the Church of St Andrew is the most important Anglo-Saxon monument in Northumberland after the crypt at

Corbridge, Vicar's Pele.

Hexham. On the south side of the churchyard is the Vicar's Pele. Built for the protection of the church during Scottish raids, this three-storey fortified tower still retains its old thick wooden door lined with iron bars. The west front has one small window, which allows light to fall on a stone book-rest where past vicars of Corbridge must have contemplated their sermons. *Corstopitum*, the Roman fort west of Cor Burn, was built in around AD90 to guard the bridge where Dere Street crossed the Tyne and to act as a supply depot for Hadrian's Wall.

## CRESSWELL TOWER

Cresswell Tower, formerly the seat of the Cresswell family, is a tower house on the Northumberland coast. The tower, with its 18th-century parapet and turret, dates from the 15th century. At one time a large house was built on to the north end of the tower, but this was demolished in the mid-19th century. This hoary old tower also has its ghost. The White Lady of Cresswell was, according to legend, the daughter of one of the old barons of Cresswell. Standing one day on the turret of the old tower, she suffered a terrible vision of seeing her lover, a Danish prince, slain on the seashore by her three brothers. She was so stricken with grief that she refused to eat, and starved to death. The tower was recently conserved to prevent it falling into further ruin. This is a now a Scheduled Monument protected by law.

**Cresswell Tower.**

**Druridge Bay.**

## DRURIDGE BAY

The firm sands of Druridge Bay, backed by a long line of dunes, sweep crescent-shaped north of Cresswell. Oak stumps, seen here in the sand at low tide, suggest an ancient submerged forest. A huge whale, washed ashore in August 1882, caused a quarrel over its ownership between the manors of Cresswell and Newbiggin. The Admiralty stepped in and, seizing the oil, they proceeded to stamp broad arrows on the bones. However, the manor of Cresswell was successful in its claim for the carcass. The jawbone went to make an archway at Cresswell Hall, a Georgian mansion pulled down in 1937.

## WINTER'S GIBBET: ELSDON

It is said that one of the best views in Northumbria is to be had from the edge of Harwood Forest, two miles south-east of Elsdon, at a point on the map named Steng Cross. However, you will find no cross on the brow of this ancient drovers' road, down which cattle were driven to market, only an 18ft gibbet. It stands as a grim reminder of the days when harsh justice was administered and passers-by suitably warned of the penalties for crime. It was here, in 1791, that the corpse of one William Winter was conveyed after being hanged at Westgate in Newcastle, and was suspended until only his skeleton remained. Winter was hanged for the murder of an old woman named Margaret Crozier. Tomlinson's 1888 *Comprehensive Guide to Northumberland* describes Winter as 'a desperate character, but recently returned from transportation', who teamed up with two vagrant women, Jane

**Winter's Gibbet, Elsdon.**

and Eleanor Clark, itinerant vendors of crocks and tinware. On the night of 29 August 1791 they encouraged Winter to break into the humble cottage known as Raw Pele and murder the old lady. It was the evidence of two young boys, Robert Hymers and Abraham Best, that brought Winter to the gallows. The previous evening, as they watched the evil trio eat their meagre meal, they became scared by the way in which the man had wielded a threatening butcher's knife. Winter was brought from Newcastle to this grim site, high on the moor, and hung in chains. The rotting body was visited by hundreds despite the stench, which was so ghastly that 'horses which travelled the road could scarcely be urged to pace the place'.

In the course of time Winter's body was replaced by a wooden effigy and later by a wooden head or 'stob'. There is a mystical belief that toothache could be cured by rubbing the affected part with wood chips cut from the gibbet. A mile to the east a small group of trees marks the site of a smithy where the cattle were shod before reaching the metalled roads.

# ELSDON: VICAR'S PELE

'For a hungry hole like Elsdon,
Aw never yet did see;
An' if aw gan back tiv Elsdon,
The de'il may carry me.'
George Chatt

**Elsdon, Vicar's Pele.**

Set in the rugged moorland of Northumbria, the isolated village of Elsdon was, in 1249, the capital of the remote Middle March. This was a lawless area, a gathering place for the Redesdale clans. So infamous was the temperament of the residents within Tynedale and Redesdale that, in 1564, a bye-law prohibited any person born within that area to be accepted as an apprentice. The spacious village green, which still has its bull-baiting stone let into the grass, once served as a pen where cattle were herded during severe weather. In about 1080 Robert de Umfraville, or Robert with the Beard, built, on the Mote Hills to the north, the castle that guarded the village. The remains of it were once the finest motte and bailey castle in Northumberland. On the fortified south front of the Vicar's Pele a shield bears the arms of the Umfravilles and above it is a helmet surmounted with a cinquefoil for the crest, supported by two wolves each holding a sword upright.

Vindolanda Roman fort.

## VINDOLANDA: ROMAN FORT

'For Imperator Caesar Marcus Aurelius Antoninus Pius Felix Augustus, greatest in Parthia, greatest in Britain, High Priest, holding tribunician power for the sixteenth time, hailed Imperator in the field twice, consul four times, Father of his Country, holder of proconsular power, out of the loyalty and devotion of the inhabitants, commander of the Fourth Cohort of Gauls.'

Building inscription of Cohors Quartae Gallorun, AD213

Vindolanda, once the frontier home of 500 Roman auxiliary soldiers, lies to the south of Hadrian's Wall. Excavations here have exposed part of a fourth-century fort and also a large civilian settlement that lay outside the walls. The identity of the first garrison that occupied Vindolanda is not known, but by 253 the Cohors I Tungrorum, an infantry unit from the Tungri tribe, were in command. They were an auxiliary unit, made up of non-citizen recruits who served for up to 25 years in exchange for Roman citizenship. Rome followed a policy of not allowing native troops to serve within their province of origin. This is a fact only recently discovered on one of the Vindolanda writing tablets.

The civilian settlement has been identified as a vicus, that is having the minimum form of self-government recognised by Roman law. The shops and dwellings had narrow frontages ranging along the street to avoid high taxes.

## HADRIAN'S WALL

'Over the heather the wet wind blows
I've lice in my tunic and a cold in my nose.
The rain comes pattering out of the sky
I'm a Wall soldier, and I don't know why.'
*Roman Wall Blues*, W.H. Auden

Built by the Emperor Hadrian in AD122 after a visit to Britain, Hadrian's Wall is the most impressive of all the monuments left by the Romans, a 73-mile physical barrier stretching across Britain from the Solway Firth to Wallsend-on-Tyne, to 'separate the Romans from the barbarians'. The construction of the wall, between AD122 and AD130, was entrusted to Aulus Platorius, legate of Britain, and the work was carried out by soldiers from three legions: VI Victrix, newly arrived in Britain from Lower Germany, XX Valeria Victrix from Chester and II Augusta from South Wales. It was a spectacular achievement. While allowing movements across the frontier to be controlled and monitored, it also segregated the irksome Brigantes in the south from the disturbing influence of the Celtic tribes in the north. When complete it consisted of 17 forts three to seven miles apart, permanent quarters for garrisons with mile castles every Roman mile (1,620 yards) and signal towers between. The wall, 20ft high to the top of the parapet, was 10ft wide with a ditch to the north as

**Hadrian's Wall.**

added protection against the Picts, and to the south a defensive earthwork ditch known as the Vallum. It is thought that about 5,000 cavalry and 13,000 infantry garrisoned it. However, 20 years after the wall was complete the legions marched northwards to build another. This second wall, made of turf, established a new frontier and was known as the Antonine Wall after Hadrian's successor Antoninus Pius.

## HOUSESTEADS FORT

Set in a commanding position on the basaltic rocks of the Whin Sill and overlooking the valley where the Knag Burn runs through the Wall in a culvert, Housesteads is the most impressive and best preserved of all the 17 forts. Its garrison, for whom the fort was built, was the First Cohort of Tungrians, later reinforced by cavalry regiments from Gaul and Spain. Among the ruins of a civilian settlement found outside the South Gate are the walls of a tavern, a shop and the turf-covered Murder House, where skeletons of a woman and a man with a sword buried in his ribs were found. The rectangular fort, with its rounded corners, covers an area of five acres.

**Housesteads Fort.**

**Halton Tower, Corbridge.**

## HALTON TOWER: CORBRIDGE

The tower, or castle, which was first recorded at Halton in 1385, is still to be seen. It stands four floors high, with corbelled turrets at its corners and a stone-vaulted basement. The Haltons, like so many at the time, were not opposed to a little reiving if the opportunity presented itself. In 1276, Sir John Halton, the Sheriff of Northumberland, was drawn into a bungled raid at Wark on Tyne. Caught in the act of 'lifting' cattle belonging to Thomas Fairburn of Wark on Tyne, he had the ignominy of being brought before his own court. The evidence was so strong that his own court could not avoid pronouncing him guilty. He escaped imprisonment by paying the aggrieved party a paltry 10 marks. In the 14th century the house came into the possession of the Carnabys, when a male member of their family married the daughter of John de Halton.

## WOODHOUSES BASTLE

'If Jesus Christ were emongest them,
they would deceave him.'
Richard Fenwick, 1597

No one has portrayed the Reivers more clearly than Bishop Leslie. 'When being taken', he wrote 'they have so much persuasive eloquence, and so many smooth and insinuating words at command, that

**Woodhouses Bastle.**

if they do not move their judges, nay and even their adversaries, to have mercy, yet they incite them to admiration and compassion.'

Bastle houses, built in the 16th century by the wealthier farmers to protect their families and livestock from reivers, were unique to the Border region. Woodhouses Bastle, at Hepple, on the north side of Harehaugh Hill, is an outstanding example of one of these houses. In 1602 William Potte, a landowner here, had his initials and date carved in the stone above the door. When the house came under attack stock would be barred in at the ground floor, while the family, occupying the upper floor, used the stone spout above the doorway for pouring hot liquids on to enemies. The vaulted ground floor and stone staircase are typical features of these fortified dwellings.

The famous Northumbrian piper James Allan was born here. Of gypsy descent he was, in 1810, condemned to death for horse-stealing; this was later commuted to life imprisonment.

## HOLYSTONE

During the Middle Ages there was a small Benedictine Priory here at Holystone. Established by one of the Umfravilles, its small sisterhood numbered from six to 27. In a grove of firs behind the Salmon Inn a path leads to the Holy Well, or Ladies' Well, a pool of crystal clear water. In 1780 it was given a low verge of stone and a stone cross was raised in the centre with the legend that, at this spot, Paulinus baptised 3,000 converts into Christianity at Easter in 627. At one end of the pool stands a statue brought from Alnwick Castle to represent Paulinus in his ecclesiastical robes.

**Holystone.**

**Kielder Water.**

# KIELDER WATER

Tucked away at the top of Northumberland, surrounded by Britain's largest forest, close to the Scottish border, lies Kielder Water, the largest man-made lake in Europe. The Kielder statistics are formidable: 25 million gallons of water are taken each day from a capacity of 44 million and it is designed to supply all the water needs of the North East. With the flooding of the upper part of the valley the reservoir, with its 27-mile shoreline, opened in 1982. Nine miles long, it covers 125,000 acres of the upper North Tyne valley and required the felling of 1.5 million trees. During its construction many people criticised this government-funded project as a white elephant. With water shortages in the south increasing, Kielder Water has now finally come to the fore. Its underground springs ensure that it always remains at high levels, regardless of the prevailing climate. Often when the south of England is forced to instigate drought measures, north-east England enjoys abundant supplies. The creation of Kielder by Northumbrian Water has made it an outstanding area for water sports, but most visitors come because of its setting against the background of Northumbrian hills. The forest is home to flora and fauna, particularly roe deer and the otter. It is one of the few places in England that is still populated by the native red squirrel. One of the best ways of appreciating the surroundings is to take the forest drive from the Visitor Centre at the western end of the lake at Kielder Castle, a hunting lodge used by the Dukes of Northumberland. This toll road covers 12 miles of forest, finishing at Byrness, a short distance from the border at Carter Bar.

Great Swinburne.

## GREAT SWINBURNE

Half a mile to the south of the hamlet of Great Swinburne is the most striking standing stone in the county. This red sandstone monolith, almost four metres in height, has incised groves running down its sides and is decorated by a series of enigmatic 'cup and ring' markings.

In 1888 Tomlinson wrote in his *Comprehensive Guide to Northumberland*, 'near the southern boundary of the park is a remarkable "Druid stone" or menhir, which is 11 feet in height, spreading out at the top like an open fern or human hand. There are one or two cup-marks upon it. It is called the Swinburn Standing-stone, and gives its name to the field just outside the castle park. Near it are three or four tumuli, or burial barrows, and a fine series of culture terraces – for the limited growth of cereals used by the primitive hunters – all within Swinburn Park'.

## MORPETH: MOOT HALL

Nestling in a loop of the River Wansbeck, some 15 miles north of Newcastle, the area where Morpeth now stands was, in mediaeval times, a minor river crossing. Standing in the middle of Oldgate and built of stone taken from the Oldgate Gatehouse in 1604 is the secular 15th-century bell tower (one of only three built in mediaeval times), from which the curfew bell still rings out at eight o' clock. The original clock, from nearby Bothal Castle, had only one hand and only four spaces between the numbers to tell the quarter hours. It was, until the early 19th century, the house of correction and the town stocks are still kept there.

**Morpeth, Moot Hall.**

**Chantry House, Morpeth.**

## CHANTRY HOUSE: MORPETH

The old Great North Road crosses the River Wansbeck on an elegant stone bridge built by Thomas Telford in 1831. By the bridge stands a small building with a recessed doorway and gabled turret, relics of the 13th-century chantry Chapel of All Saints, where the tolls were collected in mediaeval times for the bridge crossing. Morpeth Grammar School, refounded in 1552, had its origin in the old chantry school and it now houses the Tourist Information Office, a craft centre and a bagpipe museum. The museum traces the history of the pipes around the world, although Northumberland is the only English county to boast its own musical instrument, the Northumberland pipes. Blown not by the mouth but by bellows under the arm, they are less strident than Scottish pipes.

Emily Davison, the campaigner for women's suffrage who was killed by the King's horse at the Epsom Derby, is buried at the 14th-century Church of St Mary.

## BOTHAL CASTLE

Not far from Pegsworth is the lovely village of Bothal. This tiny village centres on its Saxon church and its name, derived from *bottell,* means abode. The castle, which obtained licence to crenellate in 1343, has stood on this site since Saxon times. The design, like that of Dunstanburgh, is simply that of an elongated bailey enclosed by a curtain wall and entered by a fortified gateway. If there was a

**Bothal Castle.**

motte, it has disappeared beneath the restored gatehouse tower. Mentioned as early as 1166, it came to William Bertram, baron of Mitford, by marriage. The gatehouse, rectangular in shape, has an admirable display of heraldry both on and below the merlons. On the central merlon is a stone figure holding a horn or musical instrument, while on the north-west turret a second figure is in the act of hurling down a stone. The entrance passage itself has a ribbed and pointed barrel-vault, with three blocked murder holes in the roof for annoying the invader. Only one or two of the original 14th-century windows survive at first-floor level. The transomed Perp window and drawing-room fireplace were both brought from Cockle Park Tower.

## MORPETH CASTLE

There have been two castles at Morpeth. The first was on Ha' Hill and the second on Castle Hill, a little to the north of St Mary's Church. Of the castle which was built following the Conquest, little now remains. The early history of the present castle is not easy to follow, because every time it is referred to there is uncertainty about which castle is being described; like its predecessor, it was also strengthened by a ditch. From the first it may have consisted solely as a walled enclosure and gatehouse, like Dunstanburgh and Bothal, and it is thought to have been erected by William de Greystock between 1342 and 1359. It is interesting to note that there is no portcullis on the gatehouse.

**Morpeth Castle.**

Folklore tells that Michael Scott, a famed 'wizard', would have brought the tide to Morpeth had not the courage of his assistant failed him. Following his success with the King of France, this worker of spells was summoned to Morpeth, where he instructed the inhabitants in how they could assist. After performing certain spells, a young man was to run from the mouth of the river at neighbouring Cambois to Morpeth without looking back and the tide would follow him. Pursued by the roaring tide, the young man ran as far as Sheepwash, where the noise of the water so alarmed him that he broke the spell by looking back. The advancing tide immediately stopped and the burgesses of Morpeth lost the chance of having the Wansbeck navigable between the town and the sea.

Tomlinson, in his *Guide to Northumberland*, tells us that Sheepwash is a corruption of Ship-wash; it is said that at one time small vessels sailed upstream as far as the ford or 'wash'.

## QUAYSIDE AND BRIDGES: NEWCASTLE-UPON-TYNE

Like many mediaeval cities, Newcastle developed first on its wool trade, although its fortunes were founded on coal and shipbuilding. Strategically situated on the Tyne estuary, the city soon established itself as a major seaport and it was the first to export coal. Dominating the river skyline is the graceful arc of the New Tyne Bridge, which was built in 1928 and designed as a scaled-down version of the Sydney Harbour Bridge, Australia. To replace the mediaeval nine-arched bridge across

**Quayside and bridges, Newcastle-upon-Tyne.**

the river Lord Armstrong designed the Swing Bridge. It was opened in 1876 and was, at the time, the largest of its type in the world. Centrally supported on rollers, it gives two 95ft openings to allow passage for large sea-going vessels upriver. Of the bridges that eclipse the riverside, the High Level, built to extend the Darlington–Gateshead railway to Newcastle, was the earliest. Built in 1849 to a design by Robert Stephenson, it carries both road and rail traffic.

## BLACK GATE: NEWCASTLE-UPON-TYNE

In 1157 the castle at Newcastle had seen better days when Henry II recovered it from the Scots. Its reconstruction using stone greatly strengthened the walls and new gates. By 1174 William the Lion of Scotland found the walls too strong to besiege without artillery. Work began on the great keep in 1172 and was completed some five years later at a cost of £911 10s 9d. The Black Gate, built by Henry III in 1248, was a formidable addition to the castle. Its position in the west wall enabled sentries to monitor this exposed section of wall. Said to get its name from a certain Patrick Black, it is one of the most remarkable gatehouses in England. In the mid-19th century the builders of the Victorian railway line cut ruthlessly through the castle ward and separated the mediaeval keep from the Black Gate. A picturesque two-storey house now surmounts the Black Gate and houses the library of the Society of Antiquaries of Newcastle.

**Black Gate, Newcastle-upon-Tyne.**

**The Keep, Newcastle-upon-Tyne.**

## THE KEEP: NEWCASTLE-UPON-TYNE

The Romans, in about AD120, were the first to bridge the narrow steep-sided valley of the Tyne, defending its northern abutment with a tiny fort known as *Pons Aelius*. Symeon of Durham tells us that in 1080 Robert, illegitimate son of William the Conqueror, erected a wooden stockade on this site that became known as the 'New Castle'. In 1172 a stone castle, taking five years to build, replaced this wooden structure. The architect was one Master Maurice, who also seems to have built Dover Castle. Its interior contains a staircase going straight up to the second floor, ignoring the first; this rare feature occurs only here and at Dover Castle. From the basement, vaulted by a single central column, it is possible to make one's way into the chapel. The fact that there is no direct communication with the keep, coupled with its size, suggests that this was rather the garrison chapel of the castle than the private oratory of the lord. By the mid-14th century the castle was being used as a prison.

In 1644 the keep was involved in its last fight with the Scots when Sir John Marley surrendered two days after the rest of the town had fallen. In mediaeval times Newcastle was a walled town. Walls built during the reign of Edward I were subject to a wall tax paid by the Burgesses. The town was 'fined' by Edward III for not maintaining its walls, even though the tax was collected.

## BESSIE SURTEES' HOUSE: NEWCASTLE-UPON-TYNE

Before the Tyne was embanked by the Quayside, the area known as Sandhill was nothing more than a hill of sand, which was used by the locals for recreation purposes, explaining how it got its name.

**Bessie Surtees' House, Newcastle-upon-Tyne.**

There is an old plan of Newcastle by Speed with only one house marked on the Sandhill, the Maison de Dieu. No. 41 Sandhill was home to the Banker Aubone Surtees and his family of eight children, one of whom was Bessie, a much admired local beauty.

John Scott, son of a local merchant, was a student at Oxford and during a vacation had met Bessie in the quiet village of Sedgefield. The two fell in love and on 18 November 1774 they eloped with the help of a young clothier's apprentice, James Wilkinson, who lived and worked for a Mr S. Clayton beneath the Surtees apartments. Wilkinson had hidden a ladder in the shop, and when everyone was in bed the two young men lifted it up to the first-floor window. The anxiously waiting Bessie climbed down into John's arms and hurried with him to the waiting carriage. Relays of horses then carried the young pair to the village of Blackshiel, near Dalkeith, where the Reverend Buchan married them according to Scottish law. On 19 January 1775 John and Bessie had an English marriage in St Nicholas Cathedral in the presence of their parents, but it took a further two and a half years for the stately Surtees family to entirely forgive the pair.

John later wrote: 'I eluded the vigilance of three watchmen, stationed in the neighbourhood, without a bribe; and contrived to be 60 miles from Newcastle, before it was discovered that I had left my place. My wife was a perfect heroin, and behaved with a courage that astonished me.'

The marriage interfered with Scott's prospects and they lived very frugally in London. However, once started his progress was rapid and in time he became a King's Counsel, Solicitor General, Attorney General, Lord Chief justice of the Common Pleas, with the title of Baron Eldon of Eldon, and twice Lord High Chancellor. Once, when George III was standing between Lord Eldon and Manners Sutton, the Archbishop of Canterbury, he said gravely 'I am now in a position which probably no European King ever occupied before. I am standing between the Head of the Church and the Head of the Law in my kingdom, men who ought to be patterns of morality!' The king then went on, 'Why, my Lords, did you not both run away with your wives?'

**Wooden Dolly, North Shields.**

## NORTH SHIELDS: WOODEN DOLLY

Recognised as being a part of Tynemouth, North Shields grew from a tiny fisherman's settlement nestling on the banks of the River Tyne. The monks of Tynemouth Priory established the lively early morning fish market

**North Shields.**

at the Fish Quay. In Liddle Street, close to the river, you will come face to face with a large, buxom female loitering outside the Prince of Wales public house. This brazen hussy in red, carved from oak, stands where a wooden dolly has stood since the early 1800s, when the figurehead from the collier brig *Alexander & Margaret* was first set up here.

## NORTH SHIELDS

'Bathe barefoot an' barelegg'd I trudge many a week,
With me creel on my back an' a bloom on my cheek,
I'll sell you flat fish – fine skate or fresh ling,
Pennywilks, crabs and lobsters sometimes I will bring.
Will you buy, will you buy, will you buy me fresh fish.
Will you buy, will you buy, will you buy me fresh fish.
I work hard for me living from a friend never begs,
and a huff the young ladies when they peep at me legs.
I'm healthy and handsome, quite willing and strong.
To toil for me living crying "fish" all day long.
Will you buy, will you buy, will you buy me fresh fish.'
*Cullercoates Fish Lass*

A short walk from Collingwood's monument leads to the North Shields Fish Quay, originally built by the monks from the priory, who founded the local fishing industry. North Shields has long been famous for its fish quay, but no more do the fishwives of Cullercoates wear their graphic costumes and travel with their creels all over Northumberland. At one time a Wooden Dolly to commemorate the Cullercoates fishwives stood at the end of the passage leading down to the quay, but over the years it deteriorated and it was replaced by a life-size sculpture of a fisherwoman carrying a basket and wearing a traditional shawl and full skirts. It now stands in Northumberland Square.

## PERCY CROSS: OTTERBURN

'It fell about the Lammas tide,
When the muir-men win their hay,
The doughty Douglas bound him to ride
Into England to drive a prey.'
Sir Walter Scott

Fought in the August moonlight of 1388, the battle that made Otterburn famous was little more than a glorified border raid that settled nothing. As a theme for the sonnet writers, it stands out in Border Ballads. There is some dispute as to which side of the River Otter it took place on, for

Percy Cross, Otterburn.

historians have yet to make up their minds. The accepted belief, however, has placed it west of the stream on the spur that comes down from the moors. The battle brought together Sir Henry Percy, known as Harry Hotspur, and James, Earl of Douglas. At first victory seemed to lean toward the English. Dismayed at seeing his men repulsed, Douglas seized a battle-axe and dashed into the middle of the affray. Pierced by three spears, he fell to the ground fatally wounded. An upright 'Battle Stone', about 10ft high, marks the spot where it is thought that Earl Douglas fell. Inappropriately called Percy's Cross, it stands in a grove of firs near the road. Over a thousand English were left for dead on the battlefield, and in the pursuit that followed a further 1,800 were killed and more than 1,000 wounded. On the Scottish side there were only 100 slain and 200 taken prisoner. Many of the dead were buried at Elsdon Church. According to maps of 1769, the original site of the 'Battle Stone' was a couple of hundred yards to the east, where it stood, or rather lay, until 1777 when the landowner, Mr Ellison, moved the cross because of a road diversion.

The historian, John Hodgson, maintained that the stone originated from Davyshiel Crags. His contemporary Robert White, on the other hand, argued it was from the kitchen fireplace of Otterburn Hall.

## OTTERBURN TOWER

Otterburn, famous because of its battle, is now more famed for its tweed and woollen goods. The Umfravilles, who held the manor of Redesdale, built Otterburn Tower in the 11th century to keep

**Otterburn Tower.**

**Padon Hill, Otterburn.**

in check the raiding Scots. In 1388, following the bloody battle of Otterburn, it withstood its fiercest attack from the Scots. It passed later to the Hall family, who eventually replaced it with a mansion. Its most famous owner was 'Mad Jack Hall', a well-known Jacobite rebel. Reprieved five times when tried for high treason, he was eventually executed at Tyburn. His initials are still to be seen above one of the original doors.

## PADON HILL: OTTERBURN

The Pennine way runs along the watershed between Redesdale and Tarset, passing the 12ft monument on Padon Hill. The stone pepperpot-shaped monument is situated four miles west of Otterburn. It stands exposed and isolated in moorland on top of Padon Hill with impressive views on all sides. The general belief is that the followers of the Scottish Covenanter Alexander Padon, who gave his name to the hill on which it stands, built the cairn. Without exception, each of the congregation would carry a stone to the services held on top of the hill until the work was finished. Sir Charles Morrison Bell's son Clive erected the present cairn in 1913 to commemorate the golden wedding of Sir Charles to Lady Morrison Bell of Otterburn Hall.

Blackbird Inn, Ponteland.

## PONTELAND: BLACKBIRD INN

Once the old castle of Sir Aymer de Athol and manor house of the Erringtons, the Blackbird Inn, forms part of a tower house where peace between England and Scotland was negotiated in 1244. The vaulted basement attached to the house formed part of the ancient castle of Ponteland. Douglas destroyed the house during a border raid in 1388 and Douglas, pursued by Harry 'Hotspur' Percy, took the skirmish west to the battle of Otterburn. Mark Errington, whose initials appear above a first-floor window, restored and extended the house in the 16th century. During the 17th century it fell into ruins and was roofless until 1935. Once restored, it became an inn.

## PONTELAND: VICAR'S PELE

Ponteland is a small village on the River Ponte, from which it takes its name. In the rectory garden stands a mediaeval tower that Pevsner describes as 'the ruins of a Tower House'. It is entered as 'turris de Ponteland' in the Listing of 1415 and being then the property of 'vicar eiusdem'. The construction is of rough coursed stone and there is evidence that it once had three storeys. At the base of a blocked first-floor doorway is part of a mediaeval grave cover, incised with a Celtic cross. Remains of a basement vault and a mural stair can be seen in the north wall, where a blocked first-floor doorway reuses a 12th-century cross slab in its jamb.

## SEATON DELAVAL HALL

Vanburgh was over 50 when he designed the house, thought by many to be his masterpiece, at Seaton Delaval. Built in the 16th century for the Admiral George Delaval, very little thought was given to the cost of building this showpiece. Pevsner tells us that the Admiral, in a letter to Vanburgh, wrote

**Seaton Delaval Hall.**

**Vicar's Pele, Ponteland.**

'not disposed to starve the design at all'. Built in the Palladian style, huge Tuscan columns support the portico of the central block. Burnt down twice, it stood without a roof for over 50 years, and was later used by the military in both world wars. The Delavals loved entertainment so much that they once hired the Drury Lane Theatre to produce their version of *Othello*. The House of Commons adjourned two hours early in order to attend. It took 10 years to complete, five years after the admiral's death from a fall from his horse.

## TYNEMOUTH PRIORY

For over 1,300 years Tynemouth Priory, standing within the fortifications of Tynemouth Castle and surrounded by the sea on three sides, has dominated the rocky headland at the mouth of the River Tyne. The priory succeeded an earlier seventh-century Anglo-Saxon monastery destroyed by the Danes in 865, and for more than a century it lay abandoned. During the reign of Edward the Confessor it became the fortress of Earl Tostig, brother of King Harold who was killed at the Battle of Hastings in 1066. However, before he could refound the monastery, he himself was killed at the Battle of Stamford Bridge. It was finally refounded in around 1090 by Benedictine monks from St Albans Abbey, Herefordshire,

who found it an edifying place of exile for monks who were difficult to control. Not far from the priory, just above the notorious rocks called the Black Middens, is the Collingwood Monument. Erected in 1845 by public subscription, it is a tribute to Admiral Lord Collingwood who, on 21 October 1805, led the British fleet into action at Trafalgar.

Tynemouth Priory.

## COLLINGWOOD MEMORIAL: TYNEMOUTH

High on his pedestal, the cloaked figure of Admiral Lord Collingwood greets mariners as they enter the mouth of the River Tyne. Designed by Dobson, it was erected in 1847 to commemorate the admiral who led the British fleet into the battle of Trafalgar. It was at the age of 11, 46

**Collingwood Memorial, Tynemouth.**

years before Trafalgar, that Cuthbert Collingwood entered the navy as a volunteer. He went to sea in 1761 aboard the frigate HMS *Shannon* under the command of his cousin, Captain Braithwaite.

It was on the morning of 21 October 1805 that the British fleet found themselves facing the enemy off Cape Trafalgar. The French Admiral Villeneuve drew up his fleet in the form of a crescent. As the British fleet bore down in two separate lines, Collingwood addressed his officers aboard the *Royal Sovereign:* 'Now gentlemen, let us do something today that the world may talk of hereafter.'

While on board the *Victory,* Nelson remarked, 'see how that noble fellow Collingwood carries his ship into action'. The death of Nelson gave Collingwood command of the Mediterranean fleet. Such was the state of flux in the region that he never saw England again. Repeatedly denied permission to return home, Collingwood died in March 1810 after seven years at sea.

Four guns from his flagship *Royal Sovereign* flank the steps leading to his 23ft figure.

## WALLINGTON HALL

Although the house we see today is the work of Newcastle merchant Sir William Blackett, Wallington Hall was once a border castle and then a 15th-century house. The design of the park is mainly the work of Sir Walter Calverley Blackett, who inherited the estate in 1726, while the setting of the

**Wallington Hall.**

gardens was by Capability Brown, who began his career as a gardener here. The time of Sir Walter Blackett has been described as 'the golden age of Wallington' and what had been just a wonderful country house became the centre of a flourishing and wealthy estate. Over the next 40 years Blackett employed the architect Daniel Garrett to improve the house and design a number of garden features. At one point he had a resident team of Italian plasterers at the hall to transform the principal rooms into apartments of Roman elegance. With the death of Sir Walter in 1777, his sister Julia, a Trevelyan, inherited Wallington Hall. Lady Pauline Trevelyan made the last major alterations to the house in 1885. On the advice of John Ruskin she had the central courtyard covered for a picture gallery. Since 1941 the hall has been in the hands of the National Trust. Four griffins' heads, originally belonging to the mediaeval gate at Bishopsgate, London, stand on the lawn in front of the hall.

## KIRKHARLE

A few scattered houses and a lonely church in the fields are all that Kirkharle has to show. Kirkharle is the birthplace of the landscape gardener famously known as Capability Brown. He acquired this name from his usual comment when presented with a new patch of land, that 'it had capabilities'. Here he honed the garden design skills that he would later employ. He went on to become the head gardener at Windsor and at Hampton Court before becoming responsible for laying out the famous

Kirkharle.

gardens at Kew and Blenheim Palace. 1764 saw his appointment as Master Gardener at Hampton Court and he had a hand in the design of most of the country house estates of the 18th century.

Sir William de Harle, who founded a chantry here, rebuilt the little church and its fine triple sedalia and fluted piscina in about 1336. The font, which seems too monumental for the little parish, dates from 1500 and came out of All Saints' Church in Newcastle. It bears the heraldic arms of Northumberland families, and these are copied in brass around the base.

## CHIPCHASE CASTLE

Chipchase Castle, situated in beautiful parkland on the east side of the North Tyne, is one of the most outstanding mansions in Northumberland. It is a mixture of mediaeval pele and Jacobean manor. Dating back to Saxon times, its name is derived from the old English word cheap, meaning a market, and the French word *chasse*, a hunting ground. The old pele tower is attributed to the Umfravilles of Prudhoe, who held the barony of the manor in the reign of Henry II. With the marriage of Cecily de Lisle to Walter Heron in 1348 the manor passed to the Herons of Ford. Cuthbert Heron joined the impressive Jacobean manor house to the old pele tower in 1621. The last of the Herons of Chipchase was Sir Harry, who sold the castle and estate to John Reed in 1727. Tomlinson, in his 1888 *Comprehensive Guide to Northumberland*, tells of a subterranean passage used in times of siege from the cellar to the site of the ancient village of Chipchase.

Chipchase Castle.

Haughton Castle.

# HAUGHTON CASTLE

'Last night a wind from Lammermoor
Came roaring up the glen
With the tramp of trooping horses
And the laugh of reckless men,
And struck a mailed hand on the gate,
And cried in rebel glee:
Come forth. Come forth! My Borderer,
and ride the March with me!'
*The Raiders*, W.H. Ogilvie

Haughton castle sits, in an area well known for its trout fishing, on one of the loveliest reaches of the North Tyne. The most favourable view of it is from the opposite bank at Barrasford. At one time a rope ferry carried passengers between Barrasford and the castle. The agreement for it to operate was during the reign of Henry II. The first mention of this fortress is in 1373, and in 1415 it was the 'castrum' of one John Widdrington. It still belonged to the Widdringtons in the 16th century, when it was briefly summarised as, 'an olde castell or fortress very strong, but with the roofes and floores therof bene decayed and gone'.

Haughton's history is a turbulent one, as were many of the border strongholds, and like all castles it has a ghost. The following story relates to the time when the Border Reivers or moss-troopers would carry out their attacks on English land quite legally and then return to Scotland. Archie Armstrong, the chief of his clan, had been captured by Sir Thomas Swinburne and was flung into the dungeon at Haughton having been caught 'lifting'. In the meantime Lord Cardinal Wolsey had summoned Sir Thomas to York. Well on his way, he became aware of a large key hanging from his belt. He remembered with horror the Reiver whom he'd imprisoned three days previously without food or water and, without seeing the Cardinal, Swinburne turned his horse and rode at speed back to Haughton. As he reached Durham his horse collapsed through fatigue, but by remounting another he arrived exhausted at the castle gate. On reaching the dungeon deep in the depths of the castle his worst fears were confirmed – Archie Armstrong lay dead. Maddened by hunger he had gnawed the flesh from his arms. In the years to follow, servants were afraid of working in the castle, believing that the shrieks of Archie Armstrong could still be heard coming from the dungeon. The rector from nearby Simonburn was called and, aided by a black bible, he was able to exorcise the ghost. The screams were heard again some years later when the bible was taken away for repair, but the bible was quickly returned and the shrieking stopped. Archie was at rest again.

# ST MARY'S ISLAND: WHITLEY BAY

Considered safe and remote from the excisemen, smugglers used to land their contraband on St Mary's, a small offshore island reached between tides by a short causeway that connects it to the

**St Mary's Island, Whitley Bay.**

Stephenson's birthplace, Wylam.

rocky mainland at Curry's Point. The lighthouse, erected in 1898, stands on the site of a monastic cell where traditionally the sanctuary light acted as a guide to warn passing ships of the hazardous coast. It remained in service until 1984, when it was superseded by modern navigational equipment. The island, as well as being the haunt of sea birds and grey seals, is a visitor centre open to the public throughout the year. Curry's Point is named after Michael Curry, who was hanged here on a gibbet in 1739 for the murder of the landlord of the Three Horseshoes Inn at the nearby village of Hartley.

## STEPHENSON'S BIRTHPLACE: WYLAM

George Stephenson, famous engineer and inventor of railways, was born on 9 June 1781 in a red-tiled miner's cottage at Wylam. The house, known as High Street House, stands beside the horsedrawn wagon-way that carried coal wagons, on wooden rails, from the local colliery to Lemington. As a child Stephenson was allowed to walk this line to the colliery engine house with his father's dinner. It was on this line, in 1813, that William Hedley plied up and down with his pioneering locomotive *Puffing Billy*, based on Richard Trevithick's first locomotive. In 1948, a century after Stephenson's death, the cottage was given to the National Trust by the North-East Coast Institution of Engineers and Shipbuilders. The success of the *Rocket* at Rainhill was marked a century later when, on Stephenson's birthday in 1929, the Lord Mayor of Newcastle unveiled a metal plaque on the front of the cottage with a relief of the small locomotive.

**Alnham Tower.**

## ALNHAM TOWER

The tower at Alnham, built in the late 14th century, is first mentioned in the Survey of 1541: 'At Alname be two leytle toures whereof thone ys the mansion of the vycaredge'. This stone tower lies just to the west of the church and, like most houses of its kind, the ground floor has a vaulted basement which may have been a storage area. There is no obvious access between the ground floor and the first floor; access to the upper storey may have been by means of an external ladder. Early in the 17th century the building was restored, and at this time the battlements on the top of the tower were built and replacement windows added. This is a Grade II listed building protected by law.

## ALNMOUTH

Alnmouth, situated on a narrow spur of land where the River Aln meets the sea, was originally the ancient port of Alnwick. When John Wesley came here in 1748 he called it 'a small sea-port famous for all kinds of wickedness'. In the 18th century, during the war with France, several naval encounters took place off the coast and, in September 1779, Alnmouth was attacked by the American pirate John Paul Jones, who had been cruising along the coast and fired a cannonball at the village church.

Alnmouth.

Percy Tenantry Column, Alnwick.

He missed, and the shot, weighing 68lb, hit the ground, bounced three times and crashed into a farmhouse. The village prospered as a port until a fateful storm on Christmas Day 1806, when the sea came crashing through the north-east bank and changed the course of the river. The harbour was abandoned, and Alnmouth became the small, unspoilt resort seen today. North of Alnmouth is Boulmer, a village with a seedy past. It was once the principal resort of smugglers from all parts of the Border region.

## PERCY TENANTRY COLUMN: ALNWICK

The Percy Tenantry column is the first object to greet the traveller arriving from the south. It is a Greek Doric column 83 metres high at the east end of the old town. A Percy lion stands majestically at the top of the column, on top of a base, which has a prostrate lion at each corner. Locally known as *Farmers Folly*, it was erected by the duke's grateful tenants because, following the Napoleonic Wars, their rent had been reduced by 25 per cent. The duke, far from showing gratitude for the monument to his honour, was more interested in the fact that his tenants had been able to raise the money for the monument. His reaction was to raise their rents once again.

The column, erected in 1816, was based on a design by the Newcastle architect David Stephenson. The inscription on the column reads; 'To Hugh, Duke of Northumberland, K.G. This column is erected, dedicated and inscribed by a grateful and united Tenantry. Anno Domini MDCCCXVI'.

## ALNWICK CASTLE

Described by the Victorians as the 'Windsor of the North', Alnwick Castle is the second-largest inhabited castle in England. It was the Norman Ivo de Vescis who granted the land on which Alnwick stood. Alnwick Castle (pronounced 'Annick') dates from the 11th century, and has been the stronghold of the powerful Percy family since 1309 when they succeeded the de Vescis as Wardens of the Scottish Marches. Its history is steeped in the Border wars, when the people of Northumbria depended on the Percys for survival. In 1750, the line of succession died out and the vast Percy estates were divided. Although altered over the centuries, the castle, with its octagonal and semi-circular towers, owes its outline to the Normans. The figures of soldiers on the battlements are 18th-century replacements of the mediaeval originals. Refurbished in the late 19th century in Italian Renaissance style, the principal apartments contain a magnificent collection of paintings by

**Alnwick Castle.**

Canaletto, Titian and Van Dyck. The castle is set in landscaped parkland designed by Capability Brown, a Northumbrian by birth. Each Shrove Tuesday, a mammoth football match is played between the townspeople and students studying in the town on the pastures below the castle.

## LION BRIDGE: ALNWICK

Alnwick is one of the ducal towns of Northumberland, and one is never far from the ever-present lion, a reminder of the vast domain of the house of Percy. The Percys' association with Northumberland began in 1309 when Henry de Percy bought the castle and baronetcy of Alnwick from Anthony Bek, Bishop of Durham, who had acquired the land from Eustace de Vercis. In 1337 Henry, the fourth Lord Percy, became the 1st Earl of Northumberland, a title held by the Percys until the 17th century. Not the least of Alnwick's sights is the battlemented Lion Bridge, where on the parapet the lion of the Percy family defies all who enter the town from the north. It was designed in 1773 by the Scottish architect Robert Mylne.

**Lion Bridge, Alnwick.**

## HARDY MUSEUM: ALNWICK

For 135 years the House of Hardy has been famous for the manufacture of fine fly-fishing equipment. The company's origins date back to 1872, when William Hardy set up his business as a gunsmith. A year later his brother John James joined him. William and John's fascination with angling changed the direction of their partnership and their hobby became a profession, making them global leaders in their field. Rods were made initially of lancewood, hickory and greenheart, but by 1880 bamboo had arrived and been added to the range. The company was the first to invent a system for building rods in hexagonal form from bamboo, and in 1891 the first Hardy 'Perfect' reel was patented, which is still made today. Since 1873 all Hardy rods and reels have been hand built by time-served craftsmen, and have a Lifetime Guarantee.

Hardy Museum, Alnwick.

There is an old tale linked to the building of the weir at Acklington in 1776. The salmon, which have made the Coquet the most famous of fishing rivers, were unable to swim over the weir. A certain Mr Buckland, while watching the salmon vainly attempting to leap the weir, made the promise of a ladder to assist them. Later he put up a notice on the weir that reads as follows:

'Notice to Salmon And Bull Trout!

No road at present over this weir. Go down stream, taking the first turn to the right, and you will find good travelling water up stream, and no jumping required.'

F.T.B.

At the opening of the season, the first salmon to be caught in the River Coquet is presented to the Duke of Northumberland.

## ANCROFT; VICAR'S PELE

Established by the monks of Lindisfarne in the 12th century, Ancroft was one of the four chapelries in Islandshire, a district in Northumberland that belonged to the County Palatine of Durham. The original Norman Church of St Anne comprised only a nave and chancel, but in the 14th century a tower, more military in character than ecclesiastical, was attached. Built into the nave of the church for the protection of the parson and his flock, it blocked the 12th-century doorway. Entry to the

**Ancroft, Vicar's Pele.**

tower was then only via the church, with a spiral staircase giving access to the upper floors. In the years when plague swept Ancroft, infected people were taken to a nearby field known as Broomie's Huts and a bower of broom was placed over them. When they died their bodies were burned with the broom. The church was restored in 1869, when the nave was lengthened, the chancel rebuilt and a vestry added. The bell-cote on the roof contains two bells, one of which was taken from John Wesley's chapel in London.

## BAMBURGH CASTLE

Crouched on a basalt crag within sight of Holy Island, Bamburgh Castle is often used by film-makers as a backdrop for historical romances. Mediaeval in appearance, it rises in brooding grandeur to dominate both the village and coast, with only the empty dunes and cold North Sea beyond. It was built over a Saxon well, dug in the basalt to a depth of 70ft, which gave water, 'sweet to the taste and pure to the sight'. After the departure of the Romans, Bamburgh became the capital of the powerful Northumbrian kings who ruled from the Firth of Forth to the Humber. But Northumbria's power faded, and the castle was sacked by the marauding Vikings. The Northumbrian chronicler, Symeon of Durham, wrote early in the 12th century, 'In the same year the pagans from the northern regions came with a fleet of ships to Britain like "Stinging Hornets" and, spreading on all sides like fearful

Bamburgh Castle.

wolves, they robbed, tore and slaughtered, not only beasts of burden and sheep and oxen, but also even priests and deacons, and companies of monks and nuns.' The site of a fort in 547, it was given by King Ethelfrith (the Twister) to his wife Bebba and in 1164 it was decided to build a new keep, which was erected by 1170 at the cost, it is recorded, of £4. It was thought to be impregnable, until, in 1464, after a sustained bombardment by Edward IV's artillery, it earned the dubious honour of being the first castle ever to be shelled into submission. With its broken walls and shattered roof it soon fell to the elements. In Tudor times Bamburgh was reported ruinous and decayed. Early in the 18th century it was acquired by Nathaniel Liewe, Bishop of Durham, one of the richest and most powerful churchmen of the time. On his death he left the castle as part of a charitable trust which included a free school, an infirmary with its own dispensary and a free lending library for the use if the poor. The castle was sold in 1894 to Lord Armstrong, the Victorian inventor, who restored it in the Gothic manner. It now houses the Armstrong Museum, with its wonderful collections of china, porcelain, paintings, furniture, arms and armour.

## GRACE DARLING MEMORIAL: BAMBURGH

Grace Horsley Darling, daughter of William Darling, keeper of the Longstone Lighthouse on the Farne Islands, was born in her grandfather's small cottage on Radcliffe Road, Bamburgh in 1815. Although born on the mainland, she lived her early years in a small cottage on Brownsman Island. In 1826, Brownsman having closed down, the Darling family moved to Longstone, the farthest

**Grace Darling Memorial, Bamburgh.**

island, to look after the lighthouse there, but while the whole family were involved in keeping the light lit, only the father was paid. It was from Longstone, in September 1838, that she and her father courageously rowed their tiny open boat half a mile through mountainous seas to rescue nine survivors of the stricken steam packet *Forfarshire*, which had run aground on the vicious Harcar rocks. Grace was honoured by the nation for her heroic actions in the rescue, and medals were struck to commemorate the event. Sadly, despite the attention of the best doctors, she died of consumption four years later at her sister's house, aged 26. She is buried with members of her family in the churchyard. The Victorian Gothic monument was erected in 1893 to replace the original memorial which, because of erosion, was moved into the church.

## ROYAL BORDER BRIDGE: BERWICK-ON-TWEED

Among Berwick's more familiar sights are its three great bridges, which span the Tweed and connect it to Tweedmouth, south of the estuary. The most spectacular is Robert Stephenson's Royal Border Bridge, one of the finest pieces of railway architecture to be found anywhere in the country. Built for the railway in 1847 as the 'last act of the Union' it is a magnificent viaduct of 28 arches high above the river, bearing the main East Coast line. Queen Victoria and Prince Albert opened the bridge on 29 August 1850. The River Tweed provides good fishing for both salmon and trout, and is classed as Scottish water so rod licences are not required, despite the fact that you must have a permit that can be bought at a tackle shop.

**Royal Border Bridge, Berwick-on-Tweed.**

**Ravensdowne Barracks, Berwick-on-Tweed.**

# RAVENSDOWNE BARRACKS: BERWICK-ON-TWEED

Berwick is the northernmost town in England and the only English county north of the River Tweed. Further north than many places in Scotland, it was once independent of both, having a special status as a free borough which required special mention in Acts of Parliament until 1746. Its position at the mouth of the Tweed, facing the river rather than the sea, made it an important trading centre and port. When it finally became attached to the English Crown in 1482 it had changed hands 13 times. Ravensdowne Barracks was built between 1817 and 1821 in response the town's objections to billeting the 600 soldiers of the garrison in local taverns. Designed by Vanbrugh, architect of Blenheim Palace and Castle Howard, it became the first purpose-built infantry barracks in England and now houses the museum of the King's Own Scottish Borderers, telling the history of the regiment from 1689. A little known fact, as far as records show, is that it is still at war with Russia in the Crimea, having been specifically listed as declaring hostilities in 1854 and having been left out of the peace treaty signed in 1856.

**Flodden Field, Branxton.**

# FLODDEN FIELD: BRANXTON

'Lo! bursting from their common tomb,

The spirits of the ancient dead

Dimly streak the parted gloom

With awful faces, ghastly red:

As once, around their martial king,

They closed in death-devoted ring,

With dauntless hearts, unknown to yield;

In slow procession round the pile

Of heaving corpse, moves each shadowy file,

And chaunts in solemn stain the dirge of Flodden field.'

*Border Minstrelsy*, 1834

Gracing the summit of Piper's Hill on Branxton Moor is a tall Celtic cross of Aberdeen granite set upon a rough cairn. Unveiled in 1910, the inscription reads, 'Flodden 1513, to the brave of both nations'. It marks the spot where James IV of Scotland fell at the battle of Flodden Field. Fought on 9 September 1513, this was no border scuffle but a fierce engagement, linked to greater happenings in Europe. In the summer of 1513 Henry VIII crossed the Channel with his army to honour a treaty that promised support to France or Spain should either country attack the other.

Taking advantage of the weakened army at home, James sought to aid France by invading England with great force. Having inflicted losses on the English at Norham, Wark and Etal, he took up an impregnable position on Flodden Hill near to Ford Castle, where he established his headquarters. On 9 September, shortly before dawn, a hastily recruited army led by the ailing Earl of Surrey marched north-west to counter the invasion. The battle began at four in the afternoon with an artillery cannonade. Confronted by English archers, billmen and wielders of battle-axes, the Scots were quickly surrounded, and no quarter was asked or given. By nightfall, when the English victory was secured, the King himself was dead, slain in hand-to-hand fighting, and around him lay the bodies of over 9,000 Scots and 5,000 English. Every family in Scotland had to mourn one or more of its members. The banner of the dead Scottish king was hung in triumph over the shrine of St Cuthbert in Durham Cathedral.

## BRINKBURN PRIORY

Brinkburn Priory is situated about four miles south-east of Rothbury on a small peninsula formed by the River Coquet. The learned antiquarians, Hutchinson and Grose, were both struck with admiration on viewing its ruins. Hutchinson remarked, 'This is the most melancholy and deep solitude, chosen for a religious edifice, I ever yet visited'. Grose replied 'it has a sober and solemn majesty not always found in buildings more highly decorated'. Grose adds that perhaps it may owe part of this to its romantic situation, which is 'the most proper in the world for retirement and meditation'.

**Brinkburn Priory.**

The church is all that remains of the Augustine priory founded in around 1135 by William de Bertram. At the time of the suppression of the monasteries in England, 10 black canons, or canons regular of the order of St Augustin, inhabited Brinkburn Priory. Its annual revenues were valued at £68 19s 1d according to Dugdale and £77 according to Speed.

Hidden as the priory is at present, it was more so in ancient times, when a dense forest covered the whole of the neighbourhood. In the days of border

**Beadnell Tower.**

warfare, raids often disturbed the priory. On one occasion the monks, believing they had escaped the Scots, rang the bells in jubilation. This euphoric summons guided the raiders to the sanctum that they had carelessly missed.

The Brinkburn bells, legend has it, were sent to Durham after the suppression of the monastery. Being of no great size they were despatched to their new destination in the charge of some men on horseback. They were lost when attempting to ford the river at Font, which was in high flood at the time, and only recovered miraculously afterwards through the prayers of the canons.

There is a legend that in a shady nook nearby, between the foxgloves and other flowers they loved, is the burial place of Northumbrian fairies.

## BEADNELL TOWER

Sheltering behind the sand dunes, the small village of Beadnell boasts an inn that was once a pele tower. The building, now known as the Craster Arms, lies at the centre of the village and contains the remains of a mediaeval tower house that form the rear half of the main building. Measuring some 9 metres by 7 metres, it is built of large, roughly squared stone. The basement, divided into two by a cross wall, is vaulted and has a newel staircase and an original fireplace. Such towers were built as a defence against Reivers right up to the 16th century. The earliest reference to it is in the will of Thomas Forster in 1587, when he left it to his son. The name of Beadnell is thought to derive from the name 'Bedewine'.

## CARTER BAR BORDER CROSSING

It is very bleak high up on this ridge, as may be assumed from the answer given by an old carrier, who had been asked if he did not find it so: 'Hoot, man, hoot; the very de'il himsel' wadna bide

**Carter Bar border crossing.**

**Cartington Castle, Cartington.**

there half an hour unless he was tethered". From the lay-by on the crest of the ridge at Carter Bar you can to stop and savour some of the finest scenery in Northumberland, the vast hills of the Cheviots – a natural frontier between England and Scotland. Cheviot itself rises to a height of 2,676ft above sea level. It is a broad-backed mountain with a plateau for a summit. Today's rambler will smile at the fears expressed by Daniel Defoe when climbing the mountain in 1728. Accompanied by a guide and several companions, he feared that there would not be room for all of them to stand on the top. In *A Tour through Great Britain* he writes, 'the height began to look really frightful, for I must own, I wished myself down again. We were the more uneasy about mounting higher, because we all had a notion that when we came to the top we should be as just as on a pinnacle, that the hill narrowed to a point, and we should only have only enough room to stand, with a precipice every way around us'. This area was once part of the lawless Middle March. Wardens of the Marches from either side of the border met at regular intervals to settle disputes and enforce Border Laws.

## CARTINGTON CASTLE: CARTINGTON

There are records that show the people at Cartington paid tax in 1296 and all through the 14th century. It is first mentioned in old documents of the 13th century when a small share of land was held by John le Viscount. This mediaeval castle, built for the Cartington family, was at first a walled enclosure with four corner towers. When it was finally completed a tower house was to replace one of the turrets and this formed the heart of the castle throughout the mediaeval period. All around the tower house there are traces of what appear to be the remains of orchards and other houses. This is a Scheduled Monument and a Grade I listed building protected by law.

## REIVER COUNTRYSIDE

'Nae bastles or peels
Are safe frae the de'ils
Gin the collies be oot, or the laird's awae.
The bit bairnies and wives
Gang I' dread o' their lives,
For they scumfish them oot wi' the smoutherin' strae.'
    *The Hot Trod*, Crawhall

Anyone who had their livestock stolen was allowed to cross the border, 'without let or hindrance' in an effort to recover their property for up to six days after the offences. This was known as the 'Hot Trod'. They were each required to carry a lance tipped with burning peat and follow the trail with 'hew and cry, and hound and horn'.

In 1249 the laws of the Marches, known as 'Leges Marchiarum', were written down and the borders were divided into four areas known as Marches, each controlled by a Warden. The Wardens from

**Reiver countryside.**

each country were required to meet every 40 days to sort out problems and to deal with complaints. Wardens, who were there to uphold the law, were not above indulging in some reiving themselves. Although reiving was carried on throughout the year, most activity occurred from Lammas (1 August) to Candlemas (2 February). During this time the courts were in recess.

Chillingham wild cattle.

# CHILLINGHAM WILD CATTLE

Older than the castle itself, the park, walled since 1220, has been home for over 700 years to Chillingham's famous wild white cattle. This unique herd, pure and uncrossed, is the last of a species once found in Europe's primeval forests. Descendants of the aurochs, which roamed in prehistoric times, they have white coats and black muzzles, with black tips to their horns. The herd is mostly shy but can turn quite fierce if angered, as the 18th-century wood engraver Thomas Bewick discovered while sketching one day. In *History of the Quadrupeds*, he writes, 'I was under the necessity of creeping on my hands and knees to leeward, and out of sight'. Earlier he had been chased up a tree by the dominant bull.

Edward, Prince of Wales, was wishing to chance his luck at shooting the king bull of the Chillingham herd during his visit in here in October 1872. Concealing himself in a hay cart close by, the prince was able to shoot dead the bull from a distance of 70 yards. A local poet called Robert Elliott wrote;

> 'He's a warrior ye knaa and the papers are full
> Iv a terrible encoonter he had wiv a bull!
> He slowtered the bull, but his critics will say
> That the prince was concealed in a bundle iv hay;
> An' thit it was ne feat at a' te lie hid;
> An' slowter the bull in the way that he did;
> But some folks are selfish, an' winna hear tell
> Iv ony greet feats unless done by thorsel.'

**Chillingham Castle.**

# CHILLINGHAM CASTLE

Sir Walter Scott may have used Chillingham as his setting for Osbaldistone Hall in *Rob Roy*. The Grey family has held this mediaeval fortress, complete with jousting course, dungeons and torture chamber, since they took it by force in 1245. As one of the most important families in the north they played a major role in keeping the marauding Scots at bay. Sir Thomas Grey was allowed to crenellate the castle in 1344, and a moat gave added protection. It fell to the Scottish soldiers of James IV in 1513, but was back in the hands of the Greys two days later when the Scots were defeated at Flodden Field, 12 miles away. Some 20 years later, in 1536, the Percys brought artillery to bear on Chillingham when the Greys refused to join the 'Pilgrimage of Grace' against Henry VIII's Dissolution of the Monasteries. However, by the beginning of the next century major reconstruction had been carried out. After a fire in 1803, Charles, 5th Earl of Tankerville, a title given to Sir Ralph Grey in 1409 when he stormed the castle of Tancarville in Normandy, called in Sir Jeffery Wyatville, architect to George IV. Fresh from his success at Windsor Castle, he created an Italian ornamental garden, with long avenues of trees with elaborate hedges of box and yew, on the site of the mediaeval tournament ground. During the 1930s the castle was allowed to deteriorate and fell into a state of general disrepair until Sir Humphrey Wakefield, who married into the Grey family, began an extensive restoration programme in the 1980s.

Cornhill.

## CORNHILL

Cornhill is a pleasant village on the south bank of the River Tweed opposite Coldstream. A noteworthy bridge of stone crosses the river here to Coldstream and gives pleasant views of the town. Built in the mid-18th century, the bridge was designed by John Smeaton of Eddystone Lighthouse fame. As its name implies, the village was a gathering place for grain in the old days. The red-tiled house on the Scottish side of the bridge was once a public house that was notorious for its runaway marriages. Records show that in 1819 Lord Chancellor Brougham was married to Mary Anne, eldest daughter of Thomas Eden, Baronet of Windlestone.

At one time Coldstream played a conspicuous part in history, for here, on 1 January 1660, General Monk commenced the march from Scotland to London that was so instrumental in effecting the Restoration of the Stuarts. For some unknown reason the small Post Office here, although it is in England, is regarded by the GPO as being in Scotland.

## CRASTER

The tiny fishing village of Craster is still famous for its oak-smoked kippers even though today the fish are imported from Iceland and Norway. The name Craster comes from Crawcestre, the fort of the crows, and the harbour was built in 1906 by the Craster family as a memorial to a brother who died in Tibet. The old fort has long since vanished, but the ancient Craster Tower still stands. Until

Craster.

1939 Craster shipped whinstone, which was used for building roads and kerbs. It was quarried from the area now occupied by the National Trust car park. From Craster harbour a beautiful grassy path runs beside the sea to Dunstanburgh Castle, the largest castle ruin in the county.

## DUNSTANBURGH CASTLE

On a basalt ridge overlooking Embleton Bay the shattered ruins of Dunstanburgh Castle possess splendour without rival. Built by the romantic Thomas, Earl of Lancaster and High Sheriff of England in the reign of Edward II, it is the largest castle in Northumbria. Steeped in ancient lore, he dreamed of recreating the days of King Arthur and raising a second Camelot. Sadly Dunstanburgh was barely completed when his life ended prematurely. His opposition to Edward, his royal cousin, had made him a most disloyal subject and in 1322 his army was intercepted at Boroughbridge and he was executed as a traitor six days later at Pontefract. Under John of Gaunt considerable alterations were made to strengthen the castle against the Scots. Gaunt's son then made himself King Henry IV and Dunstanburgh became a royal castle. Throughout the Wars of the Roses Dunstanburgh was a Lancastrian stronghold, changing hands no fewer than five times. During the siege of 1461 it was described as being 'stuffed with Englishmen, Frenchmen and Scots'. It fell into ruin in the 16th century and, according to legend, Sir Guy the Seeker, who failed to rescue an enchanted princess here, haunts the castle.

**Dunstanburgh Castle.**

## CRASTER TOWER

In mediaeval times Craster, or Crawcestre as it was then known, was one of nine villages in the parish of Embleton. The old fort from which the name is derived has long since vanished. In the middle of the 14th century Edmund Crasestir attached a tower to the old manor house. Mentioned in the 1415 list of border strongholds, the tower has a basement vault and newel staircase. The Craster family have now lived in the house for more than 500 years, a continuity that is now rare.

## DUDDO STONES: DUDDO

The stone circle at Duddo is to be found on rising ground north of the village towards Folklington. With their weathered furrows, these five stones vary in height from five to 10 feet and form the best-preserved megalithic monument in Northumberland. All are of red sandstone. Several burial urns have been found during excavations which suggest that at one time this was an ancient burial place.

## DUDDO TOWER

The ruins of Duddo tower are the most prominent feature on crags south of the village. The Clavering family originally built it in the early 15th century as a house and barmkin. James IV of Scotland destroyed it in 1496 but repairs to it meant that it provided protection until the late 16th century. Although only a fragment of the building is still standing, the tower had a projecting wing

**Craster Tower.**

**Duddo Stones, Duddo.**

Duddo Tower.

on the south front containing an entrance and stair. Recorded and drawn in the 19th century, the ruin gives us an important record of its appearance. This is now a Scheduled Monument and Grade II listed building protected by law.

## EDLINGHAM CASTLE

Situated in a valley on the moorland road from Alnwick to Rothbury is the straggling village of Edlingham. It was here in the 13th century that John de Edlingham built a large two-storey hall surrounded by a moat. Sir William de Felton, who added a palisade inside the moat and a gatehouse on the north side, took over the property in 1276. The gaunt ruins of the castle are beside the wooded banks of Edlingham Burn. Before 1978 the remains of Edlingham Castle were little more than one more ruined tower amid a jumble of grassy mounds. Excavations of the site between 1978 and 1982 shed light on an unknown fortified manor of which only the tower remained. The newly-exposed footings now show the entire plan of a small but complex manor or castle.

## EDLINGHAM

Edlingham is one of the five villages given to Holy Island Abbey by King Ceowulph in 737. This little village lies in a narrow green valley amid heather-covered moors. From the Alnwick road the traveller can look down and see both church and castle standing out clearly in the valley below. The Church

**Edlingham Castle.**

of St John the Baptist dates back to the middle of the 12th century. The old tower, with its massive walls and arrow-slit windows, is a harsh reminder of when it was essential to fortify even the church. It is thought that the tower was at times used as a gaol for captured Scottish moss-troopers. The porch, one of the few Norman porches in Northumberland, has a round-headed outer doorway with a barrel-vaulted roof.

Edlingham will always be remembered as being the birthplace of Margaret Stothard, a witch who was supposed to have supernatural powers. Although a mass of evidence was brought against her,

Edlingham.

she escaped the fate that befell so many witches in those days. A lengthy account of the charges is recounted in Mackenzie's *History of Northumberland*. In *Selected cases of Conscience touching Witches and Witchcraft* published in 1664 it states: 'In every place and parish, every old woman with a wrinkled face, a furred brow, a hair lip, a gobber tooth, a squint eye, a squeaky voice, a scolding tongue, having a rugged coat on her back, a skullcap on her head, a spindle in her hand, a dog or cat by her side, is not only suspected but pronounced for a witch.'

Three thousand people thought to be guilty of witchcraft are said to have died in England since the reign of Henry VIII. George II repealed the statutes against witches in 1736 by saying; 'no prosecution should in future be carried out on or against any person for conjuration, witchcraft, sorcery, or enchantment'.

## PRESTON TOWER: CHATHILL

The mediaeval Preston Tower near Chathill is one of the few survivors of 78 pele towers listed in 1415. It was built in the 1390s by Sir Robert Harbottle who, after fighting alongside Henry IV at the Battle of Otterburn, was appointed Sheriff of Northumberland and Constable of Dunstanburgh Castle. In 1513 Sir Guiscard Harbottle, a descendant, was one of six knights killed in hand-to-hand combat with James IV at Flodden Field. In 1603 two of its four towers were demolished and the stone plundered to erect farm buildings and cottages. Over the next 250 years the tower gradually fell into decay until, in 1864, Henry Baker Cresswell rescued it for the purpose of holding water tanks for his Georgian house next door. The tower still stands today and its unaltered rooms house historical maps, diagrams, ballads and stories that portray a realistic picture of the grim way of life under the constant threat of Border Reivers at the beginning of the 15th century. A bedroom and living room have been furnished as they might have been in 1400.

**Preston Tower, Chathill.**

## EMBELTON TOWER

The Old Vicarage at Embleton dates from the early 14th century and it was converted into a tower house at a cost of £40 in 1395. It is one of only three fortified vicarages in the county today. Three storeys in height, it is built in a mixture of rubble stonework and squared stone. The tower is unique in two ways: firstly, it has two vaulted rooms in the basement where other examples have only one and, secondly, it is very long. The belfry windows are like those in the tower at Ponteland, which also belongs to Merton College.

## ETAL CASTLE

In 1341 Sir Robert de Manners, troubled by border raids and feuding with bitter rivals the Herons of Ford, obtained from Edward III a licence to crenellate his mansion house at Etal. The work is thought to have been undertaken by the masons who worked on Ford Castle three years earlier. An imposing fortress, it was partially destroyed by James IV of Scotland when he invaded England in 1496, 17 years before his overwhelming defeat at Flodden in support of Perkin Warbeck, who laid claim to Henry VII's throne. In 1513 it was again seized by James, but after his demise at Flodden Field the tower was used to store the captured Scottish cannon. The entrance tower, bearing the carved arms of the Manners, is guarded by two guns from the ill-fated *Royal George,* sunk near Spithead on 29 August 1782, with the loss of over 700 lives.

**Embelton Tower.**

**Etal Castle.**

Black Bull Pub, Etal.

## BLACK BULL PUB: ETAL

The picturesque estate village of Etal, beside the River Till, consists of a single street of attractive white-painted cottages set behind flower gardens. At one end of the street is the 18th-century Manor House, while at the other are the crumbling ruins of Etal Castle. The village's most charming building is the thatched and whitewashed Black Bull Inn.

## FORD CASTLE

Odinel de Forde built the border stronghold at Ford in around 1287. The building that Sir William Heron took possession of on his marriage to the heiress daughter of Odinel de Forde, little remains. In 1338 Heron had received a license from Edward III to crenellate the Manor House and he transformed it into a courtyard castle. It was here at Ford that James IV, infatuated by the charms of the Lady Heron, spent some time before the fateful battle of Flodden Field. While James dallied, the English forces drew nearer. For two centuries the castle at Ford remained in ruins. However, between 1761 and 1764 Sir John Hussey Delaval made an attempt to rebuild the castle in the pretence of Gothic style that was stylish at the time. The result was the destruction of almost everything of interest except the two flanking towers. A century later it was altered by the Marchioness of Waterford.

## FORD

Ford owes much of its model village atmosphere to Lady Louisa, Marchioness of Waterford and bridesmaid of Queen Victoria who, in 1859, rebuilt the village as a memorial to her husband, who died after falling from his horse while hunting. Lady Waterford was a talented artist in the Pre-Raphaelite

**Ford Castle.**

Ford.

Holy Island.

style and during her long widowhood she decorated the walls of the village school with a remarkable series of Biblical scenes painted in watercolour on paper. She used the vicar and villagers as models and the murals became something of a communal village project. Tomlinson, writing shortly after the houses were rebuilt, says, 'a sweeter little village than Ford could scarcely be imagined'.

## HOLY ISLAND

In the middle of the eighth century the Venerable Bede, in his *Ecclesiastical History of the English People*, described Holy Island thus: 'As the tide ebbs and flows, this place is surrounded twice daily by the waves of the sea like an island, and twice, when the sands are dry, it becomes again attached to the mainland'. The romantic Sir Walter Scott, in his narrative poem *Marmion*, gave a more romantic image:

> 'for with the flow and ebb its stile
> Varies from continent to isle;
> Dry-shod, o'er sands, twice every day,
> The pilgrims to the shrine find way;
> Twice every day, the waves efface
> Of staves and sandaled feet the trace.'

## LINDISFARNE CASTLE: HOLY ISLAND

Using stone from the dissolved Priory, the Earl of Hertford, brother of Jane Seymour, Henry VIII's third wife, built Lindisfarne Castle as an artillery fort on the great outcrop of rock called Beblowe Crag. Although it saw little military action, its defences were breached in 1715 when the castle had, during the Jacobite Rising, a garrison of only seven men. On the evening of 10 October Lancelot Errington, a man of an old and respected Northumberland family and master of a ship lying in the harbour, assisted by his nephew, seized the castle briefly on behalf of the 'Old Pretender' James Stewart, only son of the exiled King James II. By 1820 Lindisfarne Castle's use as a fortification had ceased and the garrison had departed. It then served as a coastguard station until the latter part of the century. In 1902 it was acquired by Edward Hudson, founder of *Country Life* magazine, who commissioned Sir Edwin Lutyens to restore and convert it into a private house. The discovery of the original planting plans, found among a collection of papers at the Beatrix Farrand Library of the University of California, has enabled the National Trust to recreate the small walled garden, designed by Gertrude Jekyll 500 yards north of the castle, in accordance with her layout. Both castle and garden are now in the hands of the National Trust.

**Lindisfarne Castle, Holy Island.**

**Lindisfarne Priory, Holy Island.**

## LINDISFARNE PRIORY: HOLY ISLAND

Linked to the mainland by a mile-long causeway Holy Island, or to give it its Celtic name Lindisfarne, was in the Dark Ages the heartland of Celtic Christianity. With its windswept sand dunes, the island was ideally suited to the monastic life. On the outskirts of the village stand the sombre, weathered red sandstone ruins of the mediaeval priory. Nine saints and 16 Bishops are associated with this cradle of Christianity. Nothing remains of the first monastery, founded in 635 by St Aidan after Oswald, King of Northumbria, had given him the island. The most famous of Holy Island Bishops was St Cuthbert who, after a life of contemplation and prayer, was consecrated Bishop of this small island. The ruins to be seen today are of the mediaeval priory built by Benedictine monks from Durham who, under threat of Viking raids, abandoned it in 875, taking the body of St Cuthbert and his relics across the sands of Lindisfarne for the last time. Symeon of Durham, a 12th-century Northumbrian chronicler, gives an account of their travels: 'They wandered throughout the whole district of Northumbria, having no settled dwelling place; and they were like sheep before the faces of wolves.' With the Dissolution of the Monasteries during the reign of Henry VIII, the priory at Lindisfarne was closed.

## LINDISFARNE GOSPELS: HOLY ISLAND

The finest mediaeval manuscript was written in the late seventh century on 258 pages of vellum. The illustrations in the gospels of Lindisfarne are stunning. With over 22,000 lines of breathtaking script,

**Lindisfarne gospels, Holy Island.**

it is without doubt one of the most beautiful hand-written books in the world. A colophon was added to the manuscript in the late 10th century attributing the work to one man, a monk named Eadfrith, who became Bishop of Lindisfarne in 698. At the Dissolution it is thought to have fallen into the hands of Henry VIII's commissioners and passed to Robert Bowyer, Keeper of Records at the Tower of London. Later it was given to Sir Robert Cotton, an avid collector of ancient manuscripts and whose library formed one of the foundation collections of the British Museum. A monk by the name of Aldred translated its contents, in between the lines of the original text, into Old English when the book was at Chester-le-Street. Today the originals are kept at the British Museum, although efforts are now being made to have the gospels returned to Durham. A facsimile is on display at the parish church on Lindisfarne.

## ST AIDAN'S STATUE: HOLY ISLAND

In 635, Oswald, heir to the throne of Northumbria, prepared his outnumbered army for battle with the pagan Mercians. As he prayed, he swore that he would convert his people to the new faith if given victory. Oswald won the battle and kept his word. The missionary monk, Aidan, came to Lindisfarne to build the first Christian monastery in Northumbria. In the churchyard of St Mary the Virgin, overlooking the ruined priory, stands a larger than life statue of St Aidan. This gaunt red

**St Aiden's Statue, Holy Island.**

**St Mary's Church, Holy Island.**

sandstone figure, whose head is framed by a Celtic cross, holds in its left hand a burning torch to symbolise the light of Christianity, and a Bishop's crozier in its right. The statue, made by Miss Kathleen Parbury, a noted sculptress who visited the island over a period of years, was unveiled in the presence of her Majesty the Queen in 1958.

## ST MARY'S CHURCH: HOLY ISLAND

Weddings are a rare occurrence on Holy Island, but those that do take place retain an old and unusual tradition. After the wedding ceremony the bridal couple are greeted by a guard of honour made up of islanders, who fire shot-guns to scare away evil influences. The bride is then escorted to the so-called 'Petting Stone', sited between the chancel of St Mary's Church and the Priory. Once there, supported by two of the oldest men on the island, the bride attempts to jump over the stone without stumbling, which will ensure fertility and good fortune. Finally, the church gates are tied and the couple's release is obtained by payment of a 'toll' for the gunners' refreshments. At the reception a plate of wedding cake is then thrown over the bride's head. If it breaks, her happiness is assured.

## STORAGE SHEDS: HOLY ISLAND

One by one, as the herring industry dwindled, the huge sailing boats were upturned on the beach with their bows sawn off. Tarred and weatherproofed, they were turned into storehouses for fishing gear. In 2005 two of the three upturned herring boats, which sit to the east of the castle, were subject

Storage sheds, Holy Island.

Lobster pots, Holy Island.

to a tragic fire. The oldest, part of a 19th-century keelboat, was saved. During the months that followed, the National Trust, in conjunction with Coastal Marine at Eyemouth, was able to locate a replacement at Leith Dockyard. These upside-down storage sheds serve as a mute reminder of the once-thriving herring industry.

## LOBSTER POTS: HOLY ISLAND

In 1859 Walter White wrote in *Northumberland & The Border*; 'We saw the town under its busy aspect, preparing for the herring fishery; nets lay in heaps, or stretched out fifty or sixty yards while men and boys disentangled their mazy folds and tie the loops; around almost every door lies heaps of floats, and lines, and queer looking oil-skin garments, and ample sou'westers hang on the walls.'

At the height of the herring industry it was said that a man could, on the green above the harbour beach, walk on upturned herring barrels, up to 1,400 of them, for half a mile.

## SMALL PIPES MUSEUM; LONGFRAMLINTON

In the village of Longframlington, midway between Morpeth and Alnwick, is the small workshop of David Burleigh, maker of Northumbrian small pipes. Smaller, lighter and more versatile than their Scottish cousins, their softer, more plaintive tone makes them more suited to indoor playing. Although the Northumbrian small pipes have been around for over 300 years, more people are playing them now than at almost any time in the past. They are bellows blown, have up to six drones and 17 keys on the stopped end chanter.

**Small Pipes Museum, Longframlinton**

Twizel Bridge, Norham.

The Morpeth Gathering, held in April each year, gives an opportunity for Northumbrians, both young and old, to show off their musical talents. To this day the Duke of Northumberland still retains an official piper.

## TWIZEL BRIDGE: NORHAM

Three miles west from Norham on the east bank of the River Till stands the ruin of Twizel Castle. Twizel Bridge, dating from the early 15th century, crosses the River Till in one 90-foot span at this point. It was, until the building of Causey Arch in 1727, the largest single-span bridge in Britain, and it was here, across this bridge, that the English artillery joined with the light forces in front of Branxton on that fateful day in September.

> 'No thought was there of dastard flight;
> Link'd in the serried phalanx tight,
> Groom fought like noble, squire like knight,
> As fearlessly and well,
> Till utter darkness closed her wing
> O'er their thin host.'

Scott's poetical career may have come to a close with the *Lay of the Last Minstrel* had the publisher Archibald Constable not approached him. Constable offered 100 guineas advance for a new poem before he had seen a single line. The result was *Marmion*, which was published in 1808. 8000 copies were sold within three months.

**Norham Castle.**

# NORHAM CASTLE

Standing on the English side of the River Tweed in an area known as Norhamshire in the Palatine of Durham, Norham Castle was of major importance, as it guarded the Scottish border at one of the fords over the Tweed. Built in 1121 on the site of a motte and bailey castle, it was usually commanded by a constable appointed by the Bishop of Durham, although if the diocese was vacant this honour fell upon the king. In 1157 Henry II ordered the castles at Newcastle, Bamburgh and Wark-upon-Tweed to be rebuilt in stone. At the same time Hugh de Puiset, the Bishop of Durham, fortified the castle at Norham by building a stone keep. It withstood repeated attacks in the 13th and 14th century and was thought to be impregnable. In 1513, while Henry VIII was invading France, her old ally Scotland crossed the Tweed and laid siege to Norham with some large Scottish cannon, including 'Mons Meg', which today stands in Edinburgh Castle. At the end of two days the barbican was in ruins and the outer ward taken. The Scottish defeat at Flodden Field halted the invasion and Norham was soon back in English hands.

**Cragside, Rothbury.**

## CRAGSIDE: ROTHBURY

Set in over 1,000 acres of woodland one mile north of Rothbury the beautiful estate of Cragside, with its Gothic-style mansion, has become one of Northumbria's major tourist attractions. Built on a bare and rugged hillside for the first Lord Armstrong in 1863, it was redesigned by the great Scottish architect Richard Norman Shaw in 1883. The timber-gabled mansion is backed by a steep wooded hill, while below the gardens descend in a series of terraces and winding paths to the valley floor. In 1880, by diverting streams and digging out lakes, Armstrong developed a system to generate water power, and Cragside became the first house in the world to be lit entirely by hydroelectricity. The house contains much of the original furniture and Pre-Raphaelite paintings.

## LORDENSHAWS: ROTHBURY

High on the windswept moor above Rothbury, within the shadow of Simonside, are the Bronze Age 'cup and ring' stones of Lordenshaws. These mysterious concentric circles, linked together by linear grooves in the stones, have never been fully explained; various theories suggest maps, religious sites, fertility symbols and representations of the stars. It is unlikely, however, that their true meaning will ever be fully understood. In Northumberland virtually all the carvings are on outcrops of soft fell sandstone.

**Lordenshaws, Rothbury.**

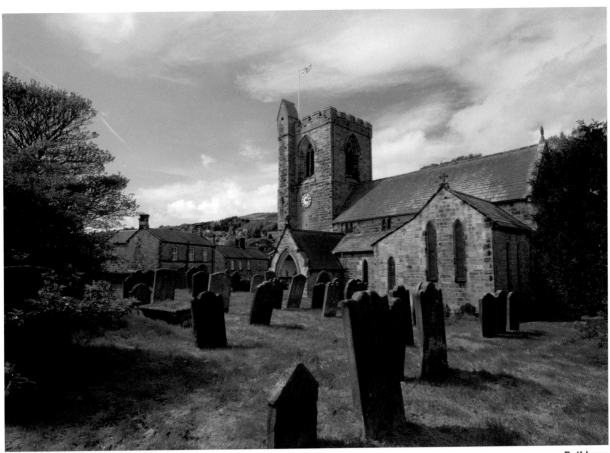

**Rothbury.**

## ROTHBURY

Rothbury, the capital of Coquetdale, lies on the north bank of the River Coquet, famous for its salmon and trout. With its wide main street, lined with old stone houses and sycamores, it is one of the most scenic villages in Northumberland. Its name, derived from the Celtic word Rhath, signifies 'a cleared spot'. The tranquillity of modern Rothbury was not always so. In past times it had a reputation for being outside the law, with fighting, gaming and drinking. Even the rector took part in poaching and was fined for a breach of the forest laws. The remains of an Iron Age hill fort can be found to the south of the town at Lordenshaws. In 1201, during a visit by King John, the town received its charter for a market and the road on which he travelled is known as Rotten Row.

## SEAHOUSES

The village of Seahouses is a continuance of North Sunderland and, until the harbour was built there in 1889, it did not exist. Describing it in 1858, Walter White said it was 'a common-looking town, squalid in places'. Today it is a much more flourishing attraction, geared up to the tourist industry. It is the usual place of embarkation for the Farne Islands. In the town there are some charming fishermen's cottages around Craster Square and superb sandy beaches stretch south towards Embleton Bay and Beadnell.

Seahouses.

Farne Islands.

## FARNE ISLANDS

The Farnes mark the easternmost reaches of the Great Whin Sill. Lying offshore to the north of Seahouses, they are divided into two main groups, the Inner and Outer Farnes, and vary in number according to the state of the tide. As one of the earliest properties of the Church, mediaeval monks used the Farnes as a retreat. St Cuthbert had a cell here; a primitive building scooped out of the living rock and lined with turf. It was here that he died in 687. The islands, now a nature reserve owned by the National Trust, provide a sanctuary for a large colony of grey seals and thousands of sea birds.

## WARKWORTH CASTLE

Shakespeare immortalised Warkworth by setting three scenes of *Henry IV* here. First built in the 12th century as a motte and bailey castle, Warkworth, which is surrounded on three sides by the River Coquet, is one of the most spectacular in Northumbria. In 1332 the castle was given by Edward III to Henry de Percy, head of one of England's most powerful mediaeval families, in part payment of expenses incurred defending the north against the marauding Scots. The Percys immediately

**Warkworth Castle.**

**Whittingham Tower.**

proceeded to improve their defences by replacing the previous building with a three-storey keep of unique shape, a cross superimposed on a square. The lower levels housed guards and servants, while the earls' quarters were above. In 1644 it again fell into Scottish hands when the Army of the Covenant attacked it. The castle has one of the vital essentials of all mediaeval romances, which in spite of their frequency in stories are in fact quite rare: an underground dungeon.

## WHITTINGHAM TOWER

'Are you going to Whittingham Fair?
Parsley, sage, rosemary and thyme.
Remember me to one who lives there,
For once she was a true love of mine.
Tell her to make me a cambric shirt
Without any seams or needlework.

When he has done and finished his work,
Parsley, sage, rosemary and thyme;
O, tell him to come and he'll have his shirt,
For once he was a true love of mine.'

Whittingham, sitting either side of the River Aln, takes on Blanchland for the title of being the perfect village. In earlier times its command of the fords, at the point where the Alnwick road joined the route north to Edinburgh, made it an important place in the Vale of Whittingham. Tomlinson tells us that the name is derived from ' the dwelling in the meadow'. In days gone by Whittingham was famous for its fair. Today the fair is far different, but for more than 100 years 'games' were held in a field by the pub on the Saturday nearest to St Bartholomew's Day.

The fortified house in the middle of the village, once the property of the Herons, was restored by Lady Ravensworth in 1845. An inscription above the door reads: 'By the munificence and piety of LADY RAVENSWORTH, this ancient tower, which was formerly used by the villagers as a place of refuge in times of rapine and insecurity, was repaired and otherwise embellished for the use of the deserving poor. A.D.1845.'

## WOOLER

Glendale, of which the town of Wooler may be considered the capital, is one of the healthiest districts in the country. However, the quiet aura of Wooler belies its violent history. Border Reivers rode this way on their forays into England. Situated about 18 miles north-west of Alnwick, this quiet market town is the best base for visits to the Cheviot Hills.

In 1791 Sir Walter Scott, while on a visit, wrote in a private letter, 'to add to my satisfaction we are amidst places renowned by the feats of former days; each hill is crowned with a tower, or camp, or

Wooler.

Yeavering

cairn; and in no situation can you be nearer more fields of battle – Flodden and Chevy Chase, Ford Castle, Chillingham Castle, and many other scene of blood are within the compass of a forenoons' ride'.

## YEAVERING

Towering above the valley floor is the Cheviot with the most congenial name, the Yeavering Bell. The best known of Northumbria's hill forts, the summit of Yeavering Bell is perhaps a better climb than the Cheviot. Its ascent can be achieved in less than an hour, over a succession of belts of bracken and heather. The top is remarkable for its enormous British camp or hill fort that embraces the whole oval summit of the hill. There was probably a gateway at each of the four compass points and, except for the west, all can be traced. Of these the south is the widest, and all have possible faint traces of a guardroom. On the summit there is a small cairn, which is supposed to be the place where the Druids of Bel-ad-Gebrin offered sacrifice to the sun. The views to the north are the hills of Flodden, and to the north-east it extends to the sea.

**Ad Gefrin, Wooler.**

## AD GEFRIN: WOOLER

In a lay-by north of Wooler, lying in the shadow of the Yeavering Bell, stands the Gefrin monument. The plaque tells us that this was the site of the Royal Township of Ad Gefrin. Bede records the fact that at the foot of the hill Edwin, first Christian king of Northumbria, had his palace. In 672 St Paulinus stayed as a guest of Edwin, whom he is reputed to have baptised in the River Glen nearby.

# GLOSSARY

**Abutment:** Meeting of an arch or vault with its support.

**Aisle:** The space alongside the nave or transept of a church.

**Arcade:** A series of arches supported by columns.

**Attic:** A top storey of a building.

**Bailey:** Courtyard area around the motte or keep of a castle.

**Barbican:** The outwork defending the entrance to a castle.

**Barmkin:** The enclosure of pele and bastle houses.

**Barrel vaulted:** Arched over like a tunnel in one direction.

**Barrow:** Burial mound.

**Barzitan:** A parapet or projecting gallery often applied to a corbelled corner turret; square or round.

**Bastion:** A projecting structure at a corner of a fortification.

**Battlement:** Fortified parapet, so that archers could shoot through the crenellations.

**Belfry:** Bell tower or chamber where the bells are hung.

**Billhook:** A long shaft with a hook for unhorsing knights.

**Bracket:** A small projecting piece of stone to support a horizontal member.

**Bronze Age:** The period in Britain from 2000 to 600BC.

**Buttress:** Support built against a wall to stabilise it.

**Cairn:** A mound of stones, usually covering a burial mound.

**Castellated:** Battlemented.

**Cinquefoil:** Ornamental window with five segments.

**Corbel:** A projecting stone block or timber support for something above.

**Crenellate:** To furnish with battlements, these have openings cut away known as crenels or embrasures.

**Crypt:** Underground room in a church.

**Curtain wall:** The wall connecting the towers of a castle, enclosing the courtyard or bailey.

**Debatable Land:** An area of land where the exact border was in dispute.

**Donjon:** Name for a castle keep.

**Drawbridge:** A hinged wooden bridge over a moat at the entrance to a castle; raised by chains or ropes.

**Dripstone:** Moulded stone projecting from a wall to protect it from water.

**Dungeon:** Castle basement or prison.

**Embrasure:** The splayed recess of a door or window.

**Flying buttress:** Wall support in the form of an arch.

**Fresco:** A painting executed on wet plaster.

**Galilee:** Chapel at the west end of a church.

**Gallery:** Balcony or gallery.

**Garderobe:** Latrine or privy.

**Gargoyle:** Carved waterspout projecting from tower.

**Gothic architecture:** A style originating in France.

**Grille:** Lattice of metal to protect a doorway or window.

**Henge:** Earthwork with surrounding bank and ditch.

**Hypocaust:** Roman underfloor heating.

**Jamb:** A vertical sidepiece or post of a doorway or window.

**Keep:** The main tower of a castle, formerly known as a donjon.

**Lancet:** Tall, slim window with pointed arch.

**Lychgate:** A roofed gateway at the entrance to a church for the entrance of a coffin.

**Machicolations:** Opening between the corbel and projecting parapet through which missiles could be dropped.

**Mason's mark:** Small geometric design in stonework, served to check output and quality.

**Mediaeval:** Belonging to the Middle Ages.

**Merlons:** The uncut part of a battlement.

**Meutriere:** An opening in the roof through which an intruder could be attacked; French, meaning murder.

**Middle Ages:** Period between the Roman Empire and the 16th century.

**Misericords:** A hinged choir stall seat which supported occupants.

**Moss-trooper:** Raider or Reiver from the Border region.

**Motte:** A steep mound of 11th and 12th-century castles.

**Motte-and-Bailey:** Norman defence system, consisting of earthen mound topped with a wooden tower within a bailey.

**Mullion:** Post dividing a window into two or more lights.

**Mural:** Relating to a wall; a mural staircase or chamber.

**Newel staircase:** One that spirals round a central post or newel.

**Norman architecture:** 11th and 12th century.

**Partizan:** A mediaeval pike.

**Perp window:** Gothic architecture 1335-c.1530.

**Pilaster:** A flat flying buttress built partly into a wall.

**Piscina:** Basin for washing communion vessels.

**Portcullis:** An iron gateway at the entrance to a castle, balanced by weights so that it could be raised or lowered at will.

**Postern:** A back door – a small gateway in the curtain wall by which secret exits could be made.

**Quatrefoil:** A window with four segments.

**Reiver:** A raider from the Border area – cut-throat, brigand or cattle-thief.

**Rustication:** Masonry with sunken or bevelled joints.

**Saxon architecture:** Pre-Norman architecture.

**Solar:** Upper living room in a mediaeval house.

**Spandrel:** The triangular space between the head of an arch and its frame.

**Squint:** Aperture in a wall to allow a view of the altar in a church.

**Transom:** A bar dividing a window horizontally.

**Vaulted:** An arched roof or ceiling.